The Salvation
School For Officers'
Library
Chicago, Illin__

A HITCHHIKER'S GUIDE TO MISSIONS

ADA LUM

InterVarsity Press
Downers Grove
Illinois 60515

36065700247837

© 1984 by Inter-Varsity Christian Fellowship of the United States of America

All rights reserved. No part of this book may be reproduced in any form without written permission from InterVarsity Press, Downers Grove, Illinois.

InterVarsity Press is the book-publishing division of Inter-Varsity Christian Fellowship, a student movement active on campus at hundreds of universities, colleges and schools of nursing. For information about local and regional activities, write IVCF, 233 Langdon St., Madison, WI 53703.

Distributed in Canada through InterVarsity Press, 860 Denison St., Unit 3, Markham, Ontario L3R 4H1, Canada.

Cover illustration: Greg Wray

ISBN 0-87784-328-7

Printed in the United States of America

Library of Congress Cataloging in Publication Data
Lum, Ada.
  A hitchhiker's guide to missions.

  Bibliography: p.
  1. Missions.   2. Missionaries—Appointment, call, and election.   3. Lum, Ada.   I. Title.
BV2061.L85   1984   266   84-19149
ISBN 0-87784-328-7

19	18	17	16	15	14	13	12	11	10	9	8	7	6	5	4	3	2	1
99	98	97	96	95	94	93	92	91	90	89	88	87	86	85	84			

19251

1

FINDING THE UNEXPECTED IN SAIGON

WHEN I INITIALLY WENT overseas as a missionary in 1962, I had been given no formal orientation. The only counsel I can remember came from an immigrant friend: "Expect the worst; hope for the best." My sending organization plunged me immediately into working not with other missionaries but with three Chinese student workers in Hong Kong where campus evangelism was sprouting all over. I was simultaneously relearning the Cantonese that I had supposedly known from childhood. Only on my days off did I begin for the first time to meet live missionaries close at hand.

A Shattering of Stereotypes
Then, in the latter half of that first term, I was asked to go to

Vietnam to relieve a missionary couple. They were going on furlough, their first in ten years, and would be officially ready for retirement after the next and supposedly last term. Later I learned that they were in the midst of their third (or was it fourth?) pioneering student work and had plans for at least ten more years.

As my colleague drove me to the Hong Kong airport for my flight out, he said, "Perhaps I'd better tell you that this couple is rather unusual."

"Yes? How unusual?"

"They are—well, you'll have to see for yourself."

Al met me at the Saigon airport. As we drove through the capital, he dutifully pointed out various historic sites. Nothing unusual about this tour guide, I thought. But as we turned into the narrow alley leading to their home, my missionary orientation began. The alley was blocked by some bicycles belonging to workers in the neighboring factory. We could not get through. In a booming voice he called out, "Hey, you in there! Get your dirty, rotten bicycles out of the way. You want me to smash them?"

I was horrified. This is a missionary? Out loud, I asked, "Won't your neighbors be offended?"

"Oh, no. They don't understand English."

"But surely they understand your tone?"

"Madame, do you or don't you want to get home?" He continued his merry whistling as the young factory men, grinning, scurried to get their bikes out of the way.

As the Ford van passed the gate into Al's home, I was in for another surprise. The house loomed up—an old, gracious two-storied one of French Colonial architecture. I quickly wondered how his frugal faith mission could possibly afford the rent—and the image—of such a house.

My stereotypes began to be shattered. I had read biographies of great missionaries like David Livingstone, Adoniram Judson and Mary Slessor. For me they were spiritual giants as well as polite, gentle people who would never shout at others, much less use seemingly insulting language with those they had come to evangelize. I always had envisioned them living in native huts, eating simple food and getting along with the minimum of Western conveniences. I also had assumed that though missionaries worked hard for the people, they kept a well-ordered program with a balanced amount of privacy.

In the few weeks before Al and Mary left for their furlough, I had to let go of many preconceptions. My missionary re-education began in earnest. They had not rented this large house for their convenience. (Their tip on how to find such a place at minimal rent is to find the neighborhood haunted house.) It was both a student center and home for themselves and others. The former servants quarters were used as a dorm for a dozen key student leaders. Except for the upstairs bedrooms, everything was open for the use of all. And even the bedrooms were often used for counseling, for Bible study groups or for the many conferences, seminars and other meetings going on all the time. They had a room full of modern equipment and other materials available for use by pastors and churches. So people were always coming and going. Sometimes I thought I was living in a three-ring circus.

Privacy? Al and Mary's life and schedule were completely exposed to the students. But by the same token, the students' lives and spiritual progress were in constant view also. Of the scores of young people and adults who came, they knew everybody by name and personal situation.

They never took days off. They both carried a full teaching load of English classes to earn money to keep the pioneering work supplied and going at full steam ahead. Al was involved in preaching engagements and evangelistic campaigns all over the country. Mary looked after the literature development and the Scripture Union reading program for churches. Amidst all of this they had constant committee meetings and personal counseling. And always they were arranging scholarships for any worthy Christian leader to be further trained abroad.

I've never been afraid of hard work, but next to them I felt absolutely idle. One day I commented, "Why do you work so hard?

Together you're doing the work of ten missionaries." Al's answer was, "We're not exceptionally hard working. It's more that most missionaries are lazy." This response was typical of his candid way of looking at any situation, and you can be sure he offended some missionaries. (But even they respected his work for God.) Their mission did not know what to do with them—or without them.

I became deeply impressed that God uses all kinds of people for his work. I learned volumes of lessons from their vigorous example and from our mealtime conversations. At times we strenuously disagreed on political issues and ways of working. But always I learned from them—often with a good deal of laughter, and never without rethinking old patterns of thought and activities.

Al and Mary were not great on prayer meetings and devotional approaches. They certainly believed in prayer. But their prayer turned to action more quickly than that of most. They were great in putting their faith into action, especially in teaching and training, and in persistent follow-up of new converts and potential leaders who could carry on the work. I would have been less direct in some social situations, and more direct in others. But they always seemed to do the opposite from me! I would have been more flexible on some biblical interpretations. They were (or really he was) strong, very strong on certain beliefs about the last days. But we heartily agreed that Jesus was returning in person.

When Saigon fell to the Vietcong in 1975, they were forced to leave South Vietnam. But they left behind trained Christians who to this day have been carrying on the work in the churches depleted of pastors.

Last week, twenty years later, I met Al and Mary again. This time it was in the United States. They were settling down to a new assignment—another pioneering work. They are in constant touch with former students and immigrants from the five countries where they have worked. Unorthodox they surely are—in more ways than I dare say here. They have not been afraid to be themselves for God's work. They represent that classic league of tough pioneer missionaries one so seldom meets from our softer, self-indulgent societies today.

They have had experiences that are absolutely unique and, though unrepeatable, still instructive for us. God does not have one mold that he uses to stamp out thousands of missionaries, all identical. Each one is different. He uses our individual personalities and gifts, our uniqueness. Sometimes he even uses the mavericks the most when they serve God as they really believe they should. But all God asks is that we be willing to turn our time, abilities and energies over to him.

Many missionaries have done just that. Many I have met, especially women, have a book within them that might ignite the final revolution for God's world mission—or so it seems from our half-humorous, half-serious conversations. Through overseas work we have learned many new things; and we have had to *un*learn just as many old patterns in order to survive. Mainly we are excited about how life in obedience to God in other cultures expands our hearts and minds, as well as his global kingdom.

Although this book is essentially my point of view, it is written somewhat on behalf of my missionary friends on every continent. I would like, if possible, to pass on the flame from those who have fired my life. I mean not only Western missionaries like these potential writers and our inimitable couple, but also national co-workers in countries where I was privileged to serve God and his people. They have goaded, inspired, encouraged and checked me from all angles, knowingly and unknowingly. How rich they have made my life—even the obnoxious ones!

Some Hard Questions
When we begin to think about missions, the basic question we should ask is not, "Should I be a missionary?" Rather the question we should ask is, "How should I be involved in God's world mission?" This question can be answered in any number of ways, and the answer may be different at one time in your life from another. We must remain constantly open to God. Let me encourage you

in this, realistically *and* positively.

First, a little realism in the form of some hard questions: Should I go overseas because it is the highest spiritual work one can do? *Is* it the highest spiritual work? Should I go because it is the humanitarian thing to do, when I live in one of the richest countries in the world? Or are such ideals patronizing? How do they relate to the actual work to be done? Should I go out of a need to be needed? A desire for self-affirmation? Nursing visions of heroic exploits for God, "natives" hungry for my every word? Should I go because my husband is a missionary and I am his wife? Even though I hate every minute of it? May I go because it combines exotic travel and Christian service? To gain experience and prestige before settling into a pastorate at home?

Or should I go because the whole thrust of the Bible is God's compassionate reaching out to his lost people? Because Jesus commanded his disciples to go into all the world? Because the early churches (as seen in Acts) were missionary churches? Because God's international mission is a logical and integral part of the gospel?

And once overseas as a missionary should I leave because the work is not what I thought it would be? Because the cultural and language differences are too great? Because my training is inadequate; because I need more education? Because my health is not up to the hardships, physically or emotionally? Because there are no marital prospects here? Because my colleagues are hard to work with? Because the people are unresponsive?

Or do I leave because the work is established and my part is done? Because of special needs of my family (spouse's health, children's education)?

May I remain because I have no real home anywhere else? Because I am too old to take on an assignment elsewhere? Because I do not want to lose my status and respect as a missionary by leaving the field? Because I do not trust the local believers to take over what I have worked hard to establish?

So, you see, missionary candidates and veterans can have quite mixed motives. Jesus' twelve disciples also had mixed motives in following him, and he knew it. He knew their good reasons and their bad ones for following him. And still he worked with them; and so he will with us, if we are willing to obey and serve him. The questions above do not have simple answers. Some of them suggest better reasons than others. But all of them, as we shall see in the following chapters, raise complex issues which should be faced in the process of considering a call to missions. And we may gain some insight into how our never-say-retire missionary couple knew when to go, when to stay and when to leave one country for another.

2

SIX WORDS
FOR A MISSIONARY

I WAS DRAWN TO TED. He was an eager, starry-eyed college senior, preparing to go to seminary the following year and wondering about missionary work after that. I detected some abilities and other potential that made me respond to him positively. I could even picture him a few years hence in a country where he might fit. But as we chatted, I discovered that he had very little idea of what a missionary does because he had only a faint notion of what a missionary is.

Finally Ted came out with the question that seemed to be for him the most important, "Where are the best openings?"

"What do you mean by the 'best openings'?" I asked.

"Well, where could I go where it wouldn't be too hard? I haven't any experience overseas, and I don't know if I'm really cut out for missionary work."

Here was a Timothy—young, open for the best that God might have for him, but hesitant and perhaps a bit naive. I recommended that he read the book of Acts thoroughly and reflect on the examples of the missionaries there. Some months later Ted wrote a long letter. He had indeed researched Acts. He had followed the travels of Peter, Philip, Barnabas, Paul and their partners as they planted and nurtured churches throughout the Roman world.

He had come to see more clearly what a missionary is. But he also had discovered something more basic and personal in the process. "I've come to the uncomfortable realization that I'm not the kind of all-out Christian those people in Acts were. . . . But I'd sure like to be. I know if I'm ever going to be a missionary, I've got to start learning how to be all-out for Christ like Paul and the rest of them."

I once met a man like the apostle Paul.

In the late 1950s, after China had been closed by the communists to missionaries and other foreigners, a Chinese brother passed through Hawaii on his way back to Peking from California. I probably took Dr. Chen sightseeing for the day to the usual tourist spots. But I can only remember asking him why he was returning to China when others were leaving if at all possible. He could easily have remained in the United States with so many job opportunities open to him as a Ph.D. in biochemistry. To go back was to walk straight into the arena of hungry lions. He simply but firmly answered in the apostle Paul's words: "I consider my life worth nothing to me, if only I may finish the race and complete the task the Lord Jesus has given me—the task of testifying to the gospel of God's grace" (Acts 20:24).

Last summer, some twenty-five years later, I unexpectedly received a brief message from Dr. Chen through a mutual friend who had been in China. He remembered our fellowship. He had indeed suffered for the sake of Christ. But Christ had not failed him, and his shared conviction with Paul was still guiding him through life and witness in China. Dr. Chen is a missionary. Very simply, a missionary is one who is sent. But there are also Buddhist missionaries and Moonie missionaries. So we have to ask, Sent by whom? Sent to whom? Sent for what? Witness, evangelist, herald, pioneer, ambassador, servant—these six biblical images can help us to see what a Christian missionary is. They naturally reflect the first-century Roman world. For us today, some of them quickly make sense; others are a bit remote. Why did the first Christians use these varied analogies for what we today call a missionary? Taking their viewpoint should broaden our understanding.

Witness. "Witness, take the stand." That is how the judge calls one to speak as truthfully and as completely as possible about an event the witness has observed. The court wants facts, not opinions. The data must be based on personal experience. The court does not require the witness to testify about things he does not know, even though such speculations might seem to round out the event.

When repeating his global commission to the eleven disciples after his resurrection, Jesus called them "witnesses": "But you will receive power when the Holy Spirit comes on you; and you will be my witnesses in Jerusalem, and in all Judea and Samaria, and to the ends of the earth" (Acts 1:8). Jesus was deliberately using an important Old Testament word once applied to the nation Israel.

"You are my witnesses," declares the LORD,
    "and my servant whom I have chosen,
so that you may know and believe me
    and understand that I am he.
Before me no god was formed,
    nor will there be one after me.
I, even I, am the LORD,
    and apart from me there is no savior.
I have revealed and saved and proclaimed—
    I, and not some foreign god among you.

You are my witnesses," declares the LORD,
"that I am God." (Is 43:10-12)
But Israel had failed to witness to the rest of the world. They
had failed to *know, believe* and *understand* his uniqueness and
his sovereign work (Is 43:10). So, how could they be his witnesses
to such glory (Is 43:21)? No conviction, no witness. Now in the
new era of grace, the same Lord God declares that we Christians
shall be his witnesses to all peoples.

Evangelist. Evangelist is not a synonym for missionary. But
their association in Scripture is very close. An evangelist is one
who tells good news. We may say, then, that the first evangelists
were those angels (messengers) who with celestial brilliance
announced the birth of Jesus to some astonished shepherds. "The
angel said to them, 'Do not be afraid. I bring you good news
of great joy that will be for all the people. Today in the town
of David a Savior has been born to you; he is Christ the Lord' "
(Lk 2:10-11). The angels were persuasive evangelists, for the
shepherds moved fast. After they had witnessed the wondrous event
for themselves, they immediately became the next evangelists,
bearing the exciting good news to others.

Once I could not imagine anyone planning to be a missionary
and not wanting to tell as many people as possible the good news
that Jesus Christ has come to bring new life for all and to start
a new era for the human race. But now I can visualize this anomaly
because I have met some "missionaries" who seemed unmotivated
to share the welcome news of Jesus. Not all missionaries have
to be totally engaged in direct evangelism. But every missionary
should at least support those who are and be involved in some
outreach to seekers. The early Christian church grew by geometric
proportions because both designated apostles and hundreds of
nameless missionaries were evangelists.

Now those who had been scattered by the persecution in
connection with Stephen traveled as far as Phoenicia, Cyprus
and Antioch, telling the message only to Jews. Some of them,
however, men from Cyprus and Cyrene, went to Antioch and

began to speak to Greeks also, telling them the good news about the Lord Jesus. The Lord's hand was with them, and a great number of people believed and turned to the Lord. (Acts 11:19-21)

Pioneer. Jesus is the great "pioneer . . . of our faith" (Heb 12:2 RSV). He blazed the way for the apostle Paul and other pioneers of his gospel. That's why the four Gospels and Acts are such great missionary books, recording their exploits for God's kingdom.

The pioneers of western North America pale by comparison. Most usually settled down in fertile country and became rich landowners. But in Acts, God's pioneers never settled down. They kept going as long as there was territory yet to be recovered for his kingdom. I was idealistic enough to be initially inspired by their examples, and I still am being inspired. Paul's example and words spoken after years of pioneering became my inspiration when I began overseas service. "And now, compelled by the Spirit, I am going to Jerusalem, not knowing what will happen to me there. I only know that in every city the Holy Spirit warns me that prison and hardships are facing me. However, I consider my life worth nothing to me, if only I may finish the race and complete the task the Lord Jesus has given me—the task of testifying to the gospel of God's grace" (Acts 20:22-24).

Herald. Herald sounds medieval, like a man one sees in a Shakespearean play. He wears a plumed hat, tights and fancy vest, blowing a trumpet to get people's attention. Then he loudly proclaims what the king wishes his subjects to do.

The word is used in the New Testament mostly in verb form and is translated "preach" (from *kēryssō*). It is one of the most common pictures of a missionary in the New Testament. Twice Paul applied the noun form—herald—to himself. "For this purpose I was appointed a herald and an apostle . . . and a teacher of the true faith to the Gentiles" (1 Tim 2:7). "And of this gospel I was appointed a herald and an apostle and a teacher" (2 Tim 1:11). Paul used the same vigorous analogy for the particular benefit of his young coworker Timothy, who at that point was discouraged enough about the ministry at Ephesus to give it all up. Paul is evidently reminding Timothy that he too has been appointed as God's herald ("preach" in 2 Tim 4:2).

The herald speaks for the one who sends him. He is responsible to reach the maximum number of the king's subjects living in that area. He communicates as clearly as possible with no attention to himself. His message has authority not because he speaks in a loud voice but because he speaks in the name of the highest authority in the land. Thereafter, it is the listeners' responsibility to obey the king's message.

Ambassador. Paul also twice calls himself and his coworkers ambassadors for Christ. "We are therefore Christ's ambassadors, as though God were making his appeal through us. We implore you on Christ's behalf: Be reconciled to God" (2 Cor 5:20). "Pray also for me, that whenever I open my mouth, words may be given me so that I will fearlessly make known the mystery of the gospel, for which I am an ambassador in chains. Pray that I may declare it fearlessly, as I should" (Eph 6:19-20).

Most people are impressed with ambassadors because they're usually quite influential. But in Paul's day they had less power than they have today. They were the king's envoys to another country for special occasions—delivering congratulations, soliciting favors, making alliances or protesting some wrong. They represented the king but had no power to negotiate. Their main task was to deliver the king's message for that occasion.[1] Paul calls himself an ambassador, not because the position was prestigious, but because for him it was both an imperative and a privilege to deliver God's special message. Even when he was in prison, he continued to be Christ's ambassador.

God still needs ambassadors to deliver his special message of reconciliation. To those men and women who, like Paul, have the passion for it, he gives authority to speak on his behalf to his subjects in another country.

Servant. Paul was the great missionary and church statesman. But he delighted to call himself a servant—literally a slave—one that belongs totally to another. More specifically he called himself Christ's slave. "So then, men ought to regard us as *servants of Christ* and as those entrusted with the secret things of God" (1 Cor 4:1). At times he seemed even to put his role as teacher under that of his role as slave: "The Lord's servant must not quarrel; instead, he must be kind to everyone, able to teach, not resentful" (2 Tim 2:24).

Yet he also considered it a unique privilege to be a servant to *others* for the sake of their salvation and their growth. "For we do not preach ourselves, but Jesus Christ as Lord, and ourselves as your servants for Jesus' sake" (2 Cor 4:5). That was not just sentimental Pauline prose, for he wrote these words to some of the most petty, quarrelsome, backbiting Christians he knew! They were young converts he had labored for through persecution and much agony. How many of us could say that we want to be servants to such ungrateful wretches? I find it much easier to be a servant to nice people. Had he not given himself first as a bondslave to Jesus his Lord, he could not have become a servant to others. Nor can we. On the other hand, if we are not serving others we cannot be serving Jesus Christ.

As St. Augustine said: "He is most truly free who is slave to Jesus Christ." And, with Paul, we have the peerless example of Jesus himself, who "did not come to be served, but to serve, and to give his life as a ransom for many" (Mk 10:45).

The Compleat Missionary

The brief study of some biblical images of a missionary have prepared us to better answer the basic question of this chapter—what is a missionary? Simply combining these images, however, does not give us a full definition. Each emphasizes one important aspect, but by itself would give a distorted view. Moreover, each presupposes certain fundamental conditions. To get to those fundamental conditions we must look to the Gospels. There we watch the Lord Jesus *personally* calling, training and sending out his select disciples to his global harvest. From this pattern, we can offer a definition: *A missionary is a prepared disciple whom God sends into the world with his resources to make disciples for his kingdom.*

A prepared disciple. To carry on his work Jesus prepared his missionary candidates for about two and one-half years before their first evangelistic assignment without him (Mk 6:7-13). After evaluation, he reinforced his teachings by even harder sayings and more intensive training before he finally left them (Mk 6:30—10:45; Jn 21:15-23).

Though we do not have Jesus' physical presence as the Twelve did, we have what they did not have—the record of the four Gospels. We have their example in the rest of the New Testament, and the permanent companionship of the Holy Spirit. We will study Jesus' training of the Twelve in chapters three and four.

When I became aware that perhaps God wanted me to be his missionary, I consciously began to prepare myself. One lasting memory of those teen-age years was cleaning our church buildings each Saturday with other members of the Girls Club. To this day I remember my bloody hands as I carelessly washed some unmovable rough glass louvers. No one else wanted to take that job because it was necessary to climb up a high ladder on one side and up to the roof on the other side. I consoled myself, "It will be worse in China." At the end of one cleaning day I saw the water hose, buckets, soap and brushes left scattered by the others who had gone home early. I had no choice but to "volunteer" to finish the cleaning. At first I felt a bit superior as a missionary in training. Then I grew resentful to the point of tears. Little did I know that, in the long haul, those days were to be the easiest part of my preparation. But it was a good start. We'll talk about hard training in chapter six.

Whom God sends. Today's disciples prepared by the Lord Jesus for his world mission should be able to hear him say clearly to them, as did the eleven, "As the Father has sent me, I am sending you" (Jn 20:21). I am no longer amazed to hear a negative response when I ask frustrated missionaries whether they went out with a sense that God had sent them. Often idealism or Christian social pressure "sent" them. Relentless 90° F. heat coupled with 95 per cent humidity is sure to melt those ideals.

It is far more important to have a deep personal conviction that God is sending you into the world, acknowledged by other responsible people, than to know which part of the world, what you should pack in your suitcase, and which make of refrigerator will best stand in a tropical climate. This kind of conviction might even cause you to leave the fridge behind. Chapter five will pursue this area.

Into the world. As long as the "world" is something remote and bizarre, something we just watch on TV, we are unperturbed. But when we come to understand the world is something that Jesus calls us to be involved in, and in a sense have some responsibility for, then we may well feel threatened. Let that threat become a challenge.

Jesus came into the world because he loved the world; yet the world hated him and rejected him. The world is full of darkness; he said, "I am the light of the world." He warned his disciples that the world would also hate them and that they would have troubles in the world, but that they could take heart because he had overcome the world. Into such a world Jesus keeps sending his prepared disciples because this is the world he died for. We will look at this question more closely in chapters seven and eight.

With his resources. "Then Jesus came to them and said, 'All authority in heaven and on earth has been given to me. Therefore go and make disciples of all nations, baptizing them in the name of the Father and of the Son and of the Holy Spirit, and teaching them to obey everything I have commanded you. And surely I will be with you always, to the very end of the age' " (Mt 28:18-20). Jesus' meaning could hardly be clearer. He who sends out workers to do his work is responsible for supplying all the needed resources to do that work. Here are the most basic resources any missionary needs: God's universal authority, his program, his instructions, his teachings, his personal companionship.

We can fully trust God to supply *all* our needs. For more than one hundred years the Overseas Missionary Fellowship (originally China Inland Mission) has operated on founder J. Hudson Taylor's conviction that "God's work done in God's way will never lack God's provisions." Thousands of missionaries testify to this in each generation.

To make disciples. For some reason I grew up as a Christian more with Mark 16:15 than with Matthew 28:18-20. So initially I was more impressed with going into *all* the world and preaching the gospel to *all* creation (Mark) than with making disciples (Matthew). Studying the continuity between the Gospels and Acts made me see what I had been missing in Jesus' commission of his disciples. For next to his work of redemption through his death, his most important work was indeed making disciples.

Acts continues that story in a different way. The disciples have become apostles/missionaries. They in turn are making disciples by preaching, teaching and training new converts. Luke crystallizes the essence of missionary work when he summarizes the first missionary tour of Paul and Barnabas.

They *preached* the good news in that city and *won a large number of disciples.* Then they *returned* to Lystra, Iconium and Antioch, *strengthening* the disciples and *encouraging* them to remain true to the faith. "We must go through many hardships to enter the kingdom of God," they said. Paul and Barnabas *appointed* elders for them in each church and, with prayer and fasting, *committed* them to the Lord in whom they had put their trust. (Acts 14:21-23)

Missionaries should underline each of these seven verbs and hang this summary on their walls.

For his kingdom. Recently in a Bible study with some professional people we studied the Lord's Prayer. Among the many excellent insights shared was the fact that it begins with God's kingdom, dips down to our very earthy needs and in full circle returns our eyes to the glory of God's kingdom. The next week one man said that this fact alone had begun to transform his perspectives on his financial ambitions. It gave a new slant to Matthew 6:33, which apparently had been slipping below his horizon: "But seek first his kingdom and his righteousness, and all these things will be given to you as well."

In the whole universe there are only two kingdoms—God's kingdom of light and life and Satan's kingdom of darkness and death (Col 1:12-13). In the end there will be only one kingdom—God's. Satan's will be totally demolished (Rev 20:10). This is why the Bible constantly appeals to people to enter into God's enduring kingdom before it is too late. And so, anywhere in the world, our mission is one of compassion: to urge men and women to decide for this ultimate kingdom where Jesus Christ supremely and joyously reigns.

3

TWO MODELS:
JESUS AND PAUL

NO EDUCATION IN MISSIONS is complete without a working knowledge of the lives and works of the world's two greatest missionaries: Jesus of Nazareth and Paul of Tarsus. They are more than great men of a great past; they should be our contemporary models for world mission. They shared, as might be expected, many similarities—both Jews, both intense, highly creative and radical thinkers. Their preparation, lifestyle, workstyle and strategy converge at many points. But there are also some interesting differences.

For instance, Jesus ministered almost exclusively in the tiny country of Palestine, a second-rate, rebellious colony of Rome. Paul traveled throughout the Roman Empire. Jesus' ministry was a brief three years, while Paul's work stretched over thirty years.

Jesus came from Nazareth, an obscure village of questionable reputation, while Paul came from Tarsus, a sophisticated and cosmopolitan city. Jesus probably had no formal education beyond the village synagogue. Paul had the highest education available, having been trained as a Pharisee and a teacher of the Law under the best Hebrew tutors, and exposed to Greek philosophy in the university town of Tarsus.

Jesus' basic work was not the same as Paul's. Jesus laid down the deep, lasting foundation on which Paul and the other apostles built. Within one generation of Jesus' resurrection the churches they planted peppered the Roman Empire.

Let us consider now some of the similarities of these two men.

Similarities in Preparation

They had a deep sense of commission. Both Jesus and Paul had an absolutely unshakable conviction that God had sent them. Jesus' first words to his disciples after the resurrection were, "As the Father has sent me, I am sending you" (Jn 20:21). In the Gospel of John, Jesus says forty times that he was sent by God. Paul identifies himself as an apostle (literally, "sent one") in the salutations of nine of his thirteen letters.

For this reason, when others opposed them, they were not deterred. Jesus told the Jewish leaders that their murderous intentions did not stop him from accomplishing God's purpose. "You are determined to kill me, a man who has told you the truth that I heard from God" (Jn 8:40).

Paul knew that some of the Corinthians rejected him, but he was still determined to be faithful to death. "For it seems to me that God has put us apostles on display at the end of the procession, like men condemned to die in the arena. We have been made a spectacle. . . . We are fools for Christ. . . . We are weak" (1 Cor 4:9-10).

Others recognized the apostleship of Jesus and Paul. The writer of Hebrews (3:1) calls Jesus the "apostle" of our confession. Luke calls Paul an apostle (Acts 14:14).

Because of this deep consciousness that their apostleship was from God, they were not filled with pride or complacency. Quite the contrary, they were humble in their Father's will.

They were well trained by life. Jesus and Paul both lived for about thirty years in relative obscurity before they entered public service for the kingdom of God. Jesus evidently spent most of his adult life as a village carpenter. Paul worked as a tentmaker. They were both recognized by others as rabbis (masters, teachers).

During this early obscurity, God was training each man, pouring into their lives all the experiences and reflections that would shape and season them for a hard, intensive life and work for his kingdom. In their ministries both men constantly drew from a rich reservoir of life experience, knowledge of Scripture and spiritual discernment.

They knew the history and the psychology of their people. They were steeped in their own Jewish history and culture, but also understood that of others. Their teachings reveal a keen understanding of human nature and personal relationships. Their vivid illustrations reflect minds accustomed to observing family and community activities.

When Paul was radically converted to Jesus Christ, his background was reinterpreted and redirected. Jesus could have been describing a rabbi like Paul when he said that "every teacher of the law who has been instructed about the kingdom of heaven is like the owner of a house who brings out of his storeroom new treasures as well as old" (Mt 13:52).

They were full of the Spirit. Luke, the first-century church historian, draws an intriguing parallel between Jesus' opening ministry in Luke 4 and Paul's first missionary trip in Acts 13. Luke strongly emphasizes that each was filled and empowered with the Holy Spirit as he began his work, and especially as he confronted evil. "Jesus, full of the Holy Spirit, returned from the Jordan and was led by the Spirit in the desert, where for forty days he was tempted by the devil. . . . Jesus returned to Galilee in the power of the Spirit" (Lk 4:1-2, 14). Right after that, in his inaugural message in Nazareth, Jesus claimed the commissioning of the Holy Spirit: "The Spirit of the Lord is on me, because he has anointed me" (Lk 4:18).

Luke records similar words about Paul. What is noteworthy here is that the leaders in the church at Antioch recognized the Spirit's activity in Paul and his partner Barnabas. "The Holy Spirit said, 'Set apart for me Barnabas and Saul for the work to which I have called them.' . . . The two of them, sent on their way by the Holy Spirit, went down to Seleucia" (Acts 13:2, 4). And like Jesus, Paul was immediately confronted with evil in the person of Elymas, a false prophet-magician. "Then . . . Paul, filled with the Holy Spirit, looked straight at Elymas and said, 'You are a child of the devil and an enemy of everything that is right!' " (Acts 13:9-10).

They each had the heart of a servant. Jesus and Paul were not only apostles, they were servants. During Jesus' last night with his disciples, none of them replaced the absent slave who customarily would have washed their dusty, smelly feet. It was not that they refused to, they simply did not think about the possibility. But Jesus did. He himself willingly assumed the status of a lowly house slave to wash their feet. This was not an isolated act. Rather this humble, menial service symbolized his whole ministry. It also previewed his greatest act on behalf of all people—his death on the cross. "Now that I, your Lord and Teacher, have washed your feet, you also should wash one another's feet. . . . No servant is greater than his master" (Jn 13:14-16).

Paul considered himself a double servant—to Jesus Christ *and* to his fellow human beings. To the Corinthians, who gave him a rough time, he said, "Though I am free and belong to no man, I make myself a slave to everyone, to win as many as possible" (1 Cor 9:19).

Similarities in Ministry
As their preparation for ministry bore many resemblances, so did their ministries. First, *their message was reconciliation to God.* The missionary is only the medium of reconciliation. God makes the appeal to alienated men and women through a go-between.

Paul's message of reconciliation is clear in 2 Corinthians 5:11-21: We have been alienated from God because of our trespasses and sins. When we are convinced that Christ, the sinless one, died for sinners, and that in faith we are brought into union with him, we are reconciled to God. "We are therefore Christ's ambassadors, as though God were making his appeal through us. We implore you on Christ's behalf: Be reconciled to God" (2 Cor 5:20). Or, in Jesus' words: "For I have come down from heaven not to do my will but to do the will of him who sent me. And this is the will of him who sent me, that I shall lose none of all that he has given me, but raise them up at the last day" (Jn 6:38-39).

They had a worldwide vision. Both Jesus and Paul considered the whole world as territory to be recovered for God. Although Jesus stayed in the area of Palestine, he clearly considered his mission to be universal. He claimed to be the Savior, bread and light of the whole world. He said to the Jews, "I have other sheep that are not of this sheep pen. I must bring them also. They too will listen to my voice, and there shall be one flock and one shepherd" (Jn 10:16). This is why he sternly corrected his disciples' misconceptions of his messiahship: not only because they envisaged him as a *political* savior, but also because they had a provincial view of him as a *Jewish* savior rather than the leader and redeemer of all peoples.

Paul traveled internationally throughout the Roman Empire. In Acts, we watch him move steadily westward from Palestine to Rome and to Spain. (Had Paul lived longer he might have even tried going to Britain, the northwest outpost of the Roman Empire.) His aim was to preach the gospel where the news of Jesus Christ had not been heard. "It has always been my ambition to preach the gospel where Christ was not known. . . . Now that there is no more place for me to work in these regions, and since I have been longing for many years to see you, I plan to do so when I go to Spain" (Rom 15:20, 23-24).

They had a strategy. Jesus and Paul had similar strategies for their ministries. They both wanted to cover as wide a geographical area as possible, to be thorough in personal ministries in each locale, and to leave behind trained men and women prepared to teach and train others. "Think globally; act locally" was their motto. Jesus moved *steadily* toward Jerusalem. His purpose was redemption for the whole human race. "As the time approached for him to be taken up to heaven, Jesus resolutely set out for Jerusalem" (Lk 9:51; and look closely at the whole structure of the Gospel of Mark).

The magnetic pull of his ultimate goal kept him from lingering too long in any one place. For instance, when the people of Capernaum eagerly sought to make Jesus stay with them longer, he said, "I must preach the good news of the kingdom of God to the other towns also, because that is why I was sent" (Lk 4:43).

But once he arrived at a place, he ministered deeply and personally to individuals and groups. His dramatic ministries to "Legion" in Decapolis and to the woman in Samaria are examples (Mk 5:1-20; Jn 4:1-28).

Paul aimed to plant churches in urban centers (in Ephesus, for example) which would radiate the gospel's power to surrounding villages and countryside (all Asia Minor). These were major cities along the famous highways and seaways linking the farflung Roman Empire. "This [teaching] went on for two years [in Ephesus], so that all the Jews and Greeks who lived in the province of Asia heard the word of the Lord" (Acts 19:10).

In a new location Paul always went to people prepared in leadership in the community. This was usually the local synagogue if there was one. Part of Paul's strategy was to win over the headman or the headwoman. If there were no experienced leaders, he and his coworkers simply kept teaching and discipling believers until they could discern who were the responsive and responsible ones to carry on God's mission in that area. Jesus' training of the Twelve is comparable to this part of Paul's ministry.

They focused on basic ministries. The basic ministries of

reconciliation are preaching to evangelize and warn, and teaching and pastoring to build up believers. In the New Testament, preaching was publicly proclaiming God's word through Jesus Christ primarily to non-Christians. Preaching had high priority as a form of evangelism, especially to reach people in pioneering areas. But in Acts we find that preaching was normally accompanied by small group or house evangelism and follow-up.

To teach is to communicate the truth systematically and clearly. Teaching must show the ethical implications of those facts that are preached. For follow-up Paul and the other apostles had assistants (catechists) like John Mark and Timothy to teach converts the basics of the gospel, the life and works of Jesus Christ. To pastor is to look after the needs of believers in order to build them up, not only as individuals but as a body also. Jesus and Paul did not separate these two roles of pastor and teacher (Eph 4:11). For how can one truly teach without pastoring, and how can one truly pastor without teaching?

They trained disciple makers to carry on the work. To preach without the clear aim of making disciples is not fulfilling Christ's Great Commission (Mt 28:18-20). Simply to increase the number of baptized church members without discipling them is not enough. Simply to get "decisions for Christ" is not obeying our Lord's mandate to make disciples.

When Jesus said, "baptizing them . . . and teaching them to observe all that I have commanded you," he was showing us *how* to make disciples. In his high-priestly prayer, Jesus said of the twelve men he had been discipling for three years, "I have taught them all that I learned from thee, and they have received it" (Jn 17:8 NEB).

Paul's priority in making disciples can be traced through his entire thirty or so years of missionary work down to his last preserved letter, 2 Timothy. This was the reason for extended stays in and return trips to newly evangelized areas. This was the reason for his many letters to young churches and young leaders. This was the reason for his daily anxieties about them.

They were men of perseverance. Luke records in Acts the occasions that Paul and his companions stayed an appreciable length of time, teaching and encouraging disciples. He spent two to three years in Ephesus, eighteen months in Corinth, two years in Caesarea (in prison), another two years in Rome (also in prison). The principle guiding Paul was: stay as long as necessary to make disciples and disciple makers for a visible local church with its own leaders and organization (Acts 14:21-23).

Jesus persevered through persecutions from his enemies, superficial responses of the crowds and gross misunderstandings of his disciples. But in the end he could say, "I have brought you glory on earth by completing the work you gave me to do. And now, Father, glorify me in your presence with the glory I had with you before the world began" (Jn 17:4-5).

They were part of a team. We often think of Paul as a strong individualist, a pioneering loner who could surmount every problem to evangelize a new region. And sometimes he did work alone. But only when he had to. Basically he worked as one member of the apostolic team. He needed their fellowship and collaboration, and said so, particularly when he was in prison. The apostolic team was a highly mobile and flexible unit with team members coming and going, crisscrossing the Roman Empire but bound together in Christ like a chain link fence.

The endings of Paul's letters are filled with warm affection and high respect for his fellow workers all over the empire. He deeply appreciated people as individuals, citing their distinctive gifts and contributions to the churches. Romans 16 is an outstanding example of this, and remarkable because at least nine and perhaps ten of the twenty-nine names are *women* coworkers.

Jesus did not have an established home base like Paul's church at Antioch, where people understood, accepted, supported and ministered to him. We should not, however, overlook the unique ministry of the women who toured with his company (Lk 8:1-3) and the hospitality of Martha and Mary (Lk 10:38). Perhaps this is why we see Jesus so often withdrawing from the crowds, as well as from his own disciples, for prayer conferences with his Father: the Father was his home base.

They knew how to cross many frontiers. Paul, the Hebrew of the Hebrews and former Pharisee, became the apostle to the Gentiles. His ministry included all races and classes of people— Jews and Greeks; Romans, Asians and Africans; slave and free; barbarian and cultured; men and women.

Jesus ministered mainly to his own Jewish people in his own country. But even within its narrow geographical borders were strongly defended frontiers of social status, personal prejudice and theological snobbishness that defied him. Think of all the frontiers Jesus had to cross when he, a provincial Galilean carpenter, debated with the doctors of the law in sophisticated Jerusalem, or conversed with a woman of bad reputation from a rejected national group!

They were men of compassion. To have compassion is to feel deeply and sympathetically for others in their sorrow and distress. Compassion is what Jesus felt when he saw a widow weeping at the funeral of her only son (Lk 7:13). Compassion made him forgive the hardened soldiers who drove the nails into his body (Lk 23:33-34).

Even when Jesus looked at the masses, his heart went out to them. "When he saw the crowds, he had compassion on them, because they were harassed and helpless, like sheep without a shepherd" (Mt 9:36). He also wept over his beloved Jerusalem, for he knew the terrible blood bath that would mark its fall in the near future (Lk 19:41).

Paul shared his Lord's compassion for people. For his fellow Jews, who hounded him all over the empire, Paul still had sorrowing love. "I have great sorrow and unceasing anguish in my heart. For I could wish that I myself were accursed and cut off from Christ for the sake of my brethren, my kinsmen by race" (Rom 9:2-3 RSV). For the Corinthians, who caused him the greatest heartache of any church in the world, he could still say, "When any man has had scruples, I have had scruples with him; when any man is made to fall, I am tortured" (2 Cor 11:29 JB).

They were men of passion. Such a ministry described above might make any missionary—veteran or candidate—cry out as did Paul himself, "Who is equal to such a task?" (2 Cor 2:16). Apart from God's grace, no one is, as Paul himself answered. This qualification is not a university or theological degree. Nor is it membership in a Bible-believing, Christ-centered and hallelujah-raising church. It is not association with a respected missionary organization. It is a passion for God himself.

Jesus' love for his Father and his just rule far outstripped any regard for his social security, his religious reputation and even his physical safety. When he fearlessly cleansed God's Temple of the corrupt practices of the ruling priestly class, his disciples were stunned. But his passion reminded them of the Scripture that described him: "Zeal for your house will consume me" (Jn 2:17).

It was this same consuming love for God that made Paul willing to go through the "dangers, toils and snares" so graphically depicted in 1 and 2 Corinthians. When I read and reflect on these passages, I feel very sad. Not because I think Paul is boasting of his sufferings, but because he is our brother, and he suffered so much for Jesus' sake, while most of us today have suffered so little.

4

FOLLOWING JESUS

LOOKING THROUGH THE SEVERAL entries for *disciple* in the Oxford English Dictionary, I was not very surprised to find a definition familiar to most of us: "a student, learner, follower of a master teacher." But it was the *first* entry that caught my interest: "one of the twelve followers of Jesus Christ." Apparently, even in secular thinking, the historic example of Jesus' relationship with the chosen Twelve helps to determine the definition of *disciple*.

How good it would be if the first entry in the record of our discipleship reflected more of Jesus' direct tutoring. *Modeling* seems to be a current buzzword among some Christians. No doubt there is a place for having a human example to follow, especially for young converts such as those who came out of the grossly pagan culture of Corinth (1 Cor 5—11, especially 11:1). And I am grateful for the superb examples I have had and still have. But often the word *modeling* sounds rather self-conscious. So does the statement often associated with it—"I'm discipling so-and-so."

The Hard Road

Recently I came across this trend in a workshop I led in the United States. The participants had read the preconference brochure describing "Discipleship: Direct Training by Jesus Christ" with subtopics on the different costs of following him. But nearly half of the participants had signed up thinking the course was on how to disciple others. They wanted to learn the failproof program I had supposedly used successfully around the world! I had none, and some dropped out after the first session.

What to do? Use the same passages (Lk 9:23-25, 57-62; 14:25-34; 2 Tim 2:1-13) but shift the viewpoints and emphasis to suit their expectations? I was tempted.

Or maybe I could carry on as planned but soft-pedal Jesus' revolutionary intent until the last day. Perhaps I could cushion the more shocking words of Jesus, like hating one's parents, and hating oneself. But my intuition whispered that many were not ready for the serious responsibility of making disciples because they had not yet themselves been discipled enough by Jesus as Lord. Through my mind flashed the troubled faces of young— and occasionally older—missionary friends I had known and sometimes counseled. Often their problems reflected a lack of direct discipling by the Lord. Then I tried to imagine the present eager young people a few years down the road. How would they be living and serving him?

No, there was no other way than to try to communicate the spirit as well as the words of Jesus concerning his kind of discipleship. Every Christian must consider and reconsider his hard sayings. If we know little or nothing about the direct disciplines of Jesus, we can hardly go further in considering our participation in his world mission.

Following a Down-to-Earth Jesus

Jesus' first command to the first disciples (and later to others) was "Follow me." Those Galileans knew what he meant: literally walk behind him. In their culture a follower did not walk beside his master. That would have been pure presumption. A common sight in a Buddhist country like Thailand is the bald, saffron-robed young men walking through the streets with their begging bowls. Later in their temple courtyards one might be able to catch a glimpse of similar novices following—carefully, humbly—behind venerable, equally bald priests.

The apostle Peter, who learned the hard way how to follow his Lord, liked this image: "To this you were called, because Christ suffered for you, leaving you an example, that you should follow in his steps" (1 Pet 2:21). We cannot follow Jesus literally as did the Twelve, for Jesus is not here bodily. But that does not release us from the command. Detailed descriptions of his earthly life have been left behind for all other disciples to follow. In fact, these historical records make it even more imperative. All but one of the New Testament references to following Jesus show that the writers had in mind the earthly Jesus. (Only Revelation 14:4 refers to a Jesus in heaven—"They follow the Lamb wherever he goes.") So when we say we follow Jesus, do we picture a Jesus based on the Gospels? Or is our picture a fanciful, nebulous one?

People who know the Gospels well can more easily conceive of following a flesh-and-blood Jesus than can those who concentrate on the Christ of the New Testament letters, where he tends to be more abstract and theologically conceived. Unfortunately, the average student with only a Sunday-school background enters college, at best, with a sixth grader's knowledge of the life of Jesus—a sprinkling of isolated miracle stories. But a systematic understanding of Jesus' earthly life makes New Testament theology more practical. This is why my usual recommendation to new disciples is to master one of the synoptic Gospels. If you have not begun to do this, you could start with Mark. It is short, concrete and fast moving. That is why Mark is often the first book of the

Bible translated in a new language group.

When you have grasped the main outline of one of the Gospels and know the highlights of Jesus' life, you will begin to see the eternal significance of particular events in his life because you see them in their proper historical context and progression to a climax. Combining this with your knowledge of the other Gospels (for instance, the complementary one of John), you will have a far richer understanding of Jesus Christ.

Discipling for Ministry

Not only is such an understanding of Jesus' person and his mission essential to your discipleship, it is *indispensable to your future ministry overseas.* Nothing else is more basic for nonbelievers and young believers. Though you will probably start by telling people a story here, a story there, eventually you must help them to know Jesus in a more factual, systematic and comprehensive way, such as through Mark. Then, through their own studies, Jesus becomes real to them for everyday choosing and doing.

And if God sends you to an oral culture, you will be challenged to be creative like Jesus, who knew how to teach such people and cause them to think for themselves about God and his kingdom—without a Bible on their laps. Refuse to be satisfied with a Sunday-school concept of Jesus. He himself has promised that his Holy Spirit, as teacher and counselor, will give you new insights. He will help you integrate these with your previous knowledge of him for a more mature understanding (Jn 14:26). Effective Bible study is a plane with two wings that gets us off the ground. One wing is reflecting on the facts in the text; the other is the Lord's gift of understanding it (2 Tim 2:7).[2]

My graduate degree was in biblical literature and theology. I had stimulating courses under excellent professors. I thoroughly enjoyed their assignments, spending hours in the library poring over theology books and commentaries. I was more than willing to stay up till the early morning hours to finish grammatical analysis of chapter after chapter in the Greek New Testament.

I do not regret one page or hour of all that. In fact, the training provided lifelong mental disciplines and a dependable biblical frame of reference for my own life and ministry to others.

But not till after graduate school did I study the life of our Lord with a group of people simply observing and interacting with what the text said about Jesus. Some friends invited me to their study group. At first, I felt vastly superior to them, none of whom had formal theological and biblical training. That group brought me down to earth fast! It was a happy humbling for me. We helped each other study the Bible less academically, more personally and practically.

During my first furlough home from overseas, I burned all my once-precious lecture notes and assignment papers (except for the still-useful New Testament theology outlines). I had thought I would eventually use them—perhaps as my own lecture notes. They represented my academic security more than did the diploma. But they had already served their purpose. Overseas I had begun to build on that invisible foundation some simpler and more practical houses for everyday living and serving with others.

Persistent Calls to Follow
Jesus called the Twelve (or at least the fishermen among them) to follow him not just once, but many times (Mk 1:16-20; Lk 5:1-11; Jn 6:66-69; Mk 10:23-31; Lk 22:24-34; Jn 21:15-22). Apparently these fishermen had returned to their lake business after Jesus' first call. They may have followed him intermittently, perhaps when it was conveniently sandwiched between good hauls of fish.

But Jesus, a persistent fisherman himself, caught them again —and again. He did not let the big ones get away. How this has encouraged me through the years of my discipleship and service! I would not be writing this book if the Lord had given me up as a lost cause after my first weak commitment—or my second or my hundredth. He keeps calling us to deeper commitment to himself. That's why I like this definition: Christians are people who give all that they know of themselves to all that they know of Jesus Christ. This definition allows infinite room for growth on both tracks.

Does this mean that every Christian disciple should be a missionary? Put that baldly, the quick, easy answer is no. For who would support them? Perhaps one-tenth of a congregation should go overseas and the remaining nine-tenths support them. Moreover, not every Christian should go overseas because in every home country unevangelized areas remain. In the United States, for example, there are growing ethnic subpopulations and increasing urban needs. Finally, the Gospels and Acts likewise show some selectivity. Jesus sent out the chosen Twelve and then later seventy-two disciples for special evangelistic work (Lk 9:1-6; 10:1-17). And as Acts 13:1-4 tells us, the church at Antioch heard the Holy Spirit instruct them to send two of their best leaders overseas. (Though I am sure their congregation numbered more than twenty.)

Some may feel relieved that such statistics get them off the missionary hook—if hook it is. But statistics are descriptions, not imperatives. Moreover, Luke throughout his book of early church history (Acts) delights in mentioning undesignated missionaries who evangelized and started churches wherever they were scattered (Acts 8:8-39; 11:19-21; 28:13-15). Other references in the New Testament letters also give evidence of churches started not by the designated apostles, but by many nameless, "nonprofessional" missionaries. In any case, the question is not "Should I be a missionary?" but "How am I to be following Jesus right now?"

But Few Are Chosen

After Jesus had been with his many disciples a year and both sides had had ample opportunity to observe each other, Jesus was ready to choose the special Twelve. They would have key leadership responsibilities in his work after he left. It was no easy choice. He prayed all night (Lk 6:12). Perhaps he was thinking about many other disciples with potential to be apostles. He was probably weighing all the pros and cons of each of the Twelve. He surely must have thought hard about Judas. Did he already detect some hint of treachery? What potential did Jesus see in him as an apostle?

Once Jesus designated the Twelve, he did not change his mind or revise his plans, even toward the end. In fact, he committed himself to teaching and training them even more carefully. He committed himself completely to them.

Jesus had many other disciples. Some he called. Others on their own initiative asked to follow him. The three candidates for discipleship in Luke 9:57-62 were representative of many who had the desire to follow him. But they were still woolly in their understanding of what discipleship really involved. By the time of the resurrection there were at least five hundred "brothers" (1 Cor 15:6). At one time, there were perhaps thousands, many of whom were merely curious, superficial freeloaders climbing on the bandwagon (Jn 6:25-34). They were nevertheless called disciples. But Jesus had ways of sifting these so that in time they themselves chose to drop out: "Upon hearing it [Jesus' teaching on total identification with him], many of his disciples said, 'This is a hard teaching. Who can accept it?' . . . . From this time many of his disciples turned back and no longer followed him" (Jn 6:60, 66).

How painful this must have been for Jesus. Immediately after that mass exit of disciples he turns to the Twelve. "You do not want to leave too, do you?"

Simon Peter answers for the group, "Lord, to whom shall we go? You have the words of eternal life. We believe and know that you are the Holy One of God" (Jn 6:67-69).

Though he presents many "hard teachings," Jesus never asks any disciple to drop out of his course, not even a Judas. He does everything he can, short of forcing us, to have us follow him more deeply into his ways. So much and so compassionately does he believe in our potential. Where are you on the road of discipleship with the Lord Jesus? Just a curious, superficial disciple like those Galilean freeloaders? Or fascinated with Jesus and perhaps even intellectually convinced like Nicodemus (Jn 3) but not yet personally committed to him and his aims? The Twelve also traveled this route. But their kind of fascination with Jesus made them follow him persistently.

Jesus said, "For many are invited, but few are chosen" (Mt 22:14).

Trouble on Jesus' Team
"Seventy-five per cent of the problems faced by missionaries on the field have to do with interpersonal conflicts with colleagues. A person may have fine job qualifications and personal talents, but be unable to complete his ministry due to inadequacies in the area of social skills."[3] This statement is disturbing because it is made by someone who has interviewed thousands of candidates and returning missionaries. Dr. LeRoy N. Johnston, Jr., is the director of missionary candidates for the Christian and Missionary Alliance and a licensed psychologist. He is working with other mission organizations on this problem. A humble way to accept its seriousness is to acknowledge that there is a seventy-five per cent chance for any of us to be entangled in such situations overseas. Or maybe you are facing it right now with other Christians in your fellowship or church.

During the first two years with Jesus, the Twelve were absorbed in learning from him and in gradually experiencing "success" (Mk 1:21—9:32). Then in the last six months before his death they began to fall into the seventy-five per cent bracket. Arguments about which of them was the greatest, and who were most deserving of cabinet posts in his coming kingdom flared up periodically (Mk 9:33-37, 38-41; 10:35-45). These continued until the very night of his arrest (Lk 22:24-30). The disciples knew little about teamwork until after his resurrection.

So it is not surprising that Jesus deliberately spent more and more time alone with them, teaching, correcting, checking, rebuking, yet all the time also encouraging them. On at least fourteen occasions between Mark 6:30 and 10:45, Jesus drew them away from public ministry for more intensive training. He knew that they could not carry on his work without unity among themselves.

I confess to a growing admiration for the worldwide work of various orders of the Roman Catholic Church. I have seen them working with the rejects of society with a compassion I wish more Protestant bodies expressed. Other orders run some of the best schools in the Third World. In some places a Roman Catholic school or retreat center is the only possible location for us to hold a student conference. And always the staff serve us with loving efficiency. Their teamwork is outstanding. They have a commitment to each other, as well as to the Lord. Protestants have the same basic theory of teamwork, but we are often short on the practice. Our individualism gets in the way. It is not enough to commit ourselves only to Jesus. We need to commit ourselves to each other for the sake of Jesus and his work.

As with the Twelve, the Lord Jesus wants to teach us how to handle our feelings of jealousy, rivalry, superiority, criticalness, and our so-called successes and achievements. If we do not learn to deal with these now, no amount of other preparation here or prayer meetings there will dissolve them.

What about those other kinds of feelings like a deep sense of inadequacy or uselessness? What about not just failure but foolish failure? Or those times when we feel rejected, defeated or blank before God, if not before others? I would not have been able to live and keep ministering without hearing Jesus repeating *my* name as he did for Simon Peter's: "Simon, Simon, Satan has asked to sift you as wheat. But I have prayed for you, Simon, that your faith may not fail. And when you have turned back, strengthen your brothers" (Lk 22:31-32). Substitute your name for Simon's name the next time you're feeling depressed. Visualize Jesus' face, gestures and tone of voice. This has been good therapy for me. (You can do the same with John 21:15-22.)

The Lord has far more confidence in us than we have in him, because he knows not only our foolish ways but also the good things that he has built into us. His Holy Spirit is living in these bodies of ours. While it is important to consider committing ourselves to Jesus Christ, it is staggering that he, God Almighty, has already committed himself to us. He says to Simon and to us, "*When* you have turned back," not "*if* you turn back." How could a foolish braggart like Simon Peter afterward firmly commit himself to others and to God's work? Because he finally understood that Jesus' commitment to him was greater than his commitment to Jesus.

Such a commitment to us will sustain us in good times and bad, at home and across cultures. But we can only truly learn of Jesus' commitment to us as we follow Jesus day by day wherever he leads us.

5

BEING CALLED, BEING SENT

IN MY FIRST YEAR IN Hong Kong, I met Ruth, an attractive and pleasant young missionary from South Dakota. Gorgeous complexion! But what really fascinated me was that she spoke perfect Cantonese with perfect humility and no self-consciousness. She was one of the sponsors for the burgeoning high-school evangelistic work. Each week she would come to the city from the New Territories for instruction in group Bible studies. She devoured everything that was taught and recommended.

Called by God
Usually in a conversation or two I can learn what a person's mission and denominational background are. But with Ruth I could not tell. There were no clues. She was engrossed with her

present work—and she was effective. My curiosity got the best of me, and one day I asked directly.

"What mission board are you with?"

"None."

Hmmm. "Who sent you?"

"God." Again, with perfect humility—no self-consciousness.

"How did you know what to do? You know—where to live, what language course to take, and all that orientation bit."

"I graduated from Bible school and knew I wanted to be a missionary to the Chinese. So I came."

"I see. Did you know anyone here?"

"No."

"How are you supported?"

"By my church."

"Ah, then they sent you."

"Yes, I suppose you could say that. Yes, God and my church sent me."

The last I heard was that God had sent her a most suitable husband, and together they are happily serving the God who sends.

Ruth is not typical. Few people can do what she did without the help of an experienced mission organization. But she illustrates what is most necessary—an unshakable sense of God's calling and sending. More common than Ruth, unfortunately, are young, disillusioned missionaries, equally attractive and pleasant when they start out. They go through a prescribed orientation course and are then sent triumphantly overseas by their church and a respectable mission organization. But they lack a deep and tested sense of call. Without such conviction, the major life adjustments and the challenges of overseas work are overwhelming. With such a conviction, they can face them and eventually be productive.

But they cannot do it alone. Few missionaries are the rugged individuals we read about in mission biographies of the eighteenth and nineteenth centuries. Individualism in the West does not necessarily produce tough character. I saw in Ruth a tested character, a tested disciple. I was impressed with her cheerful obedience to God. And even she had a strong supporting church.

Called by the Church

Strong personal ties to a home church are essential. A local church usually knows the candidate better than the mission organization. In fact, sometimes a mission organization can be more professional than personal in its relationship to candidates. On the other hand, I know missionaries who are far closer to their mission society than to their home church. This is usually because they consider their church spiritually weak. But such a relationship should not remain long. For during home leaves and especially in retirement, where will be the needed fellowship and mutual support?

Missionary candidates should have the kind of church that Paul and Barnabas had behind them in Antioch. The leaders of that church recognized and supported their call and nourished that mission partnership during their furlough (Acts 13:1-4; 14:26-28; 15:35). But note that before Paul and Barnabas were sent out, they had already served that church well (Acts 11:25-26). A tested partnership of candidate and church is essential. I would dare say that no missionary should cross a gospel frontier without the working fellowship of a church like that in Antioch.

The church at Antioch is an important model of a sending church for three reasons. The first is that we do not have enough of them, and should work harder to grow and multiply such at home. The second is that some missionary candidates may have to consider changing membership to a church that is closer to biblical standards. This change has to be weighed carefully. The third reason is that this is the kind of church missionaries should be planting and nurturing.

Acts 11:19—15:35 describes the founding and growth of the church at Antioch. We find it was an enlightened church (11:19-20), an evangelistic church (11:21-26), a growing church (11:21-26), an eager, warm church (11:22, 26), a well-taught church

(11:26; 15:35), a caring church (11:27-30), an interracial church (13:1), a well-led church (13:1), a worshiping church (13:2), a listening and obedient church (13:2-3), a missionary church (13:2-3) and a supportive church (14:26-28; 15:35).

In summary, a New Testament church is a local body of believers who are corporately obedient in every possible way to its head, the Lord Jesus. In this kind of church the godly leaders will sense the Holy Spirit guiding them as a body to recognize the calls and gifts of their members. The church should not wait for individuals to come up and say, "The Lord is leading me overseas. Would you consider supporting me as your missionary?" According to Acts, the burden should not be on the individual alone. A healthy church should be growing missionaries among its people. Leaders should watch those who are already about their Father's business. It is not necessarily the flashy young people's leader.

But I can't leave this church at Antioch without looking more closely at one of its key leaders. Barnabas is not as famous as Paul. But without him, humanly speaking, Paul may not have become a great missionary and church statesman. We need more Barnabases, who will help raise up Pauls and pick up the younger John Marks which the Pauls sometimes impatiently leave behind.

A concordance will provide you all the references you need to pursue his instructive life history. But in the same passage we have been examining (Acts 11:19—15:35), we discover the basic qualities that made Barnabas a great missionary. He was culturally sensitive ("to Greeks also," 11:20-22), spiritually sensitive ("saw the evidence of the grace of God," 11:23-24), emotionally sensitive ("was glad," 11:23), personally sensitive ("went to Tarsus to look for Saul," 11:25) and pastorally sensitive ("encouraged them . . . taught great numbers," 11:23, 26).

Most missionary candidates would be realistic to aspire to be more like Barnabas, "son of encouragement," than like Paul, the great church/missionary statesman. If they did aspire to follow Barnabas's example, and if their church were like the one at Antioch, it would recognize and support God's call for them.

Building Up Support

I have often been asked how I could take on an itinerant ministry without a home of my own. I happily answer that I have had both a supportive family and a supportive Christian community. The church where I was converted and nurtured continued to encourage me at each step of my call, my training and my early service in Hawaii. They never undertook my full financial support, as they could have. This was to help me gain a broader base of support from other churches and individuals. I think this was healthy, for I was able to keep in touch with different kinds of churches and friends. Their combined prayer support has been immeasurable, to say nothing of their monetary giving.

The better people know you as a good friend and tested servant of the Lord while you're with them, the stronger will be their prayer and financial support for you overseas. Regular prayer and financial support go hand in hand. It is hard to pray fervently for missionaries and their needs without being touched to give, if possible. And when people give money to support people overseas, they are surely more likely to follow that with prayers, so that the gift is multiplied in effect like the lad's fish and bread in the hands of Jesus.

Individuals and student groups may contribute to a missionary's financial and prayer support, even though such individuals do not take the place of local church support. Student groups are temporary in their support because they disband after three or four years. Nevertheless, I have appreciated their enthusiastic and personalized support through the years. The relationship gives opportunity for mission education for young people and excellent contacts with aspiring missionaries. And even after a group has disbanded, individuals have often continued their loyal support. I am still amazed to have the generous support of several men and women who have prayed for me daily and given regularly for many, many years. If that does not make a person feel responsible, humanly speaking, I do not know what else can.

It is dangerous to depend on any narrow, individual base of support. An extreme case of this happened a few years ago. A mission organization was created by one Christian's generosity. It was innovative, daring to do some things that traditional mission organizations would not dare to do. Its creativity caught my attention because I knew some people in it. I saw them blossom in what they had been dreaming of doing for years. Then suddenly the philanthropist died. His estate was left in the hands of family members and others who did not have the same missionary sentiments.

Certain churches in North America have been famous for their annual missionary conferences and unusually huge missionary budgets, sometimes exceeding their local budget. They certainly have set an example. Their very reputation has reminded others that keeping a missionary on the field may be far more important than the need to redecorate the social hall. Where impressive budgets and conferences are paralleled with personal relationships with their missionaries, there one finds an especially healthy church.

But a church with an "ordinary" budget is not necessarily less of a missionary church. I think of one small church that has been supporting me financially for all the years I have been overseas. At first their giving was not spectacular, but it has increased year after year, even when their local financial statements dipped into red ink. Their love also comes through regular letters of encouragement, the kind that inspire any missionary to take at least a few minutes to answer their request for "some current specific items for prayer."

Called to Ministry
With Barnabas and the Antioch church in view, let us consider the ministry we are called to. Does every missionary preach, teach and pastor, or "just evangelize"? The answer is yes and no.

When missionaries work in teams that together cover these basic ministries, the answer is no. The wise agency makes assignments so that individual gifts complement one another for the purpose of making disciples and growing disciple makers in the churches. In time these teams should be more and more a healthy mixture of missionaries and local leaders and workers.

On the other hand, the pioneering missionary, working alone in an unevangelized area, should preach, teach, pastor and evangelize. This "area" may be a whole village or tribe. But often it is an enclave, that is, a certain cultural group or social segment or even one individual within a country or town. Then the missionary naturally will not worry whether he has all the necessary gifts. The one concern is to bring people to Jesus and build up his body. Therefore the missionary will exercise any of these ministries as needed. Then he will discover that the Holy Spirit has given him the very gifts that were needed.

I am always amazed and delighted in Malaysia when I meet brothers and sisters who were brought to Christ in a remote village or town that was evangelized by lay Christian doctors, teachers and other professional people. Some years ago a group of young graduates from the Christian fellowship at the University of Singapore surveyed what was then the Federation of Singapore and Malaysia. They dedicated themselves to planting churches in towns and villages where there was no witness to Christ. They scattered themselves to various parts of the country in obedience to Christ's Great Commission. They were usually alone in their vision and work. Today you can find churches and Christians in these places because those nonprofessional missionaries—alone—preached and evangelized, taught and pastored in order to make disciples.

I have never fancied myself a pioneer. I avoid the role whenever I possibly can. I have always been relieved that some of my coworkers were clearly gifted with a pioneering constitution. Yet again and again I have been thrown into situations where I either had to do the work of a pioneer or let precious opportunities slip by. Eventually I saw that not every missionary needs to be a pioneer. But all missionaries must have a measure of the pioneering spirit.

This is one way to stay young. And die young.

That goes for evangelism too. I never considered evangelism my gift, especially when I saw coworkers bring people to Christ every day, or so it seemed. In the first years after that glorious time of theological training, I wanted to pass on those glorious outlines to others. When evangelistic projects came up, I edged away, telling myself that my gift was teaching, counseling or whatever else could cover my fears. One day in the Philippines the national director of the student work exhorted our staff team, "Not all of us have the gift of evangelism like Jesse" (who was tremendously effective and upon whom we unconsciously depended for most of the evangelism). "But we all have the responsibility of evangelism." That put me on the right track.

God's Gentle Guidance

For twenty years I thought that God was leading me to China. This came from no special vision. It was simply logical. First, China contained a quarter of the world's population and therefore had the greatest number of non-Christians to be evangelized. Second, China was my parents' home country, and therefore my cultural "home." From ninth grade onward I geared everything for missionary work there. I planned university and graduate courses accordingly. My lifestyle was shaped by this aim.

But I never got to China. By the time I finished my formal studies, the bamboo curtain had descended. I was not disappointed. I was secretly relieved: maybe it had been only a teen-ager's idealism. I could serve him just as well at home in Hawaii. So I settled into a church and student ministry there.

Happy I was, but China and world mission remained on my mind. God was gently nudging me in all kinds of ways. Ten years later I went to Hong Kong to help with the new student work bursting at the seams. I thought this would at last fulfill my commitment to God to work among the Chinese. Though it was not in mainland China as I had originally thought, I was prepared to serve the Chinese anywhere for the rest of my life. I never seriously considered any other people.

While still in Hong Kong, I was asked to help the new student work in another country nearby, and then another and another after that. At first, with each new assignment I would think that this surely is the country where I will finally settle down. Near the end of that first term, my supervisor, David Adeney, asked me to consider still another country for my second term. I said no, I should return to where I was, as it was clearly God's will for me. At that point he replied as politely as usual, "Ada, that's exactly what you said about the last three countries you've been in."

I remember feeling a bit stupid. The greater impact, however, was something else. It suddenly dawned on me that maybe, just maybe, God had an itinerant ministry for me in the various countries of Southeast Asia where he was raising up student movements. Little did I know that I would serve in still other Asian countries, and eventually on other continents. Who would have dreamed up such a fantastic mission? Not I. Only God could have. And apparently he told David Adeney and Stacey Woods, our general secretary.

If God had earlier revealed such an itinerant ministry, I would have said neither yes nor no. I simply would not have been able to comprehend it at all. Had I been mistaken about China for twenty years? Had God been misleading or teasing me? No, on both counts. He leads us according to our understanding at any given time. If I had not thought, prayed and planned specifically in terms of going to China, I might not have prepared for missionary work at all. My discipleship would not have been oriented to Jesus' lordship over the whole world.

Had I been disobedient for those ten years in Hawaii? By God's grace I can also say no. It is hindsight that enables me to see his broader and deeper preparation for me (1) to experience different types of Christian ministries, (2) to learn how to work with people of various ages, (3) to know and be supported by a wider Christian community, and (4) to go through deep personal struggles so that I would live in greater dependence on him.

I share this personal history to show how incredibly wise and gentle is the Lord who leads his servants step by step, year by year, vision by vision, and—sometimes—nation by nation. We can only know how trustworthy he is when we are leadable.

6

GETTING READY
TO GO

WHEN EILA WAS PREPARING to go overseas, she asked our general secretary, an experienced traveler, what to take. His wife had always done his packing, and all he could think to say was, "Your passport, health documents showing you have a cholera shot, and a mosquito net." Of course, Eila had to pack a few other things in her luggage and ship some heavier goods ahead. But the far more important preparation for an overseas mission begins long before the packing and shipping of our worldly goods.

Broad Fellowship
Recently I was in a covenant group, one of many in a large Presbyterian church in northern California. I had been tempted to welsh on my promise to accompany my host to this weekly

fellowship (in order to work on this chapter!). But I'm glad I went. It was a holy experience to be received warmly and to fit naturally into the group. Their love absorbed my newness.

Our ages ranged from twenty-four to eighty-five. A bright young Japanese *sansei* (third generation in the United States) was at the young end, and a retired biology professor tipped the other end. Between them ranged the rest of us—five women of various racial and economic backgrounds. Our marital status also ran a gamut—widowed, divorced, still married and negotiable. We studied Acts 8, sharing our insights and eventually sharing our questions and hang-ups in life. It soon became clear that we represented various levels of spiritual growth. Yet there was a beautiful oneness of spirit: everyone wanted to learn from God through his Word and through one another.

I was especially touched by the professor's humble participation. He asked genuine questions about the text that led to fruitful discussion. He was almost childlike in wanting to know more about following the Lord Jesus. Later I learned that he had returned only a few years ago to this Presbyterian church after following his wife to her Christian Science church since they first married. Then I better understood his eager participation. He was joyfully back on the road of discipleship with the Lord Jesus at eighty-five, and making up for lost time!

This brings us to the first path of preparation for ministry. Every disciple of Jesus should be in such a sharing, caring small group with other believers. (This is assuming that all believers should belong to a local church, though I am discovering that not all young Christians like to make such commitments.) Pastoral care and support should come not only from the professional church staff. The New Testament is full of exhortations for all of us to nurture and support one another. Colossians 3:16 is representative: "Let the word of Christ dwell in you richly as you [plural] teach and admonish one another with all wisdom."

A missionary candidate should therefore try to belong to a *mixed* group if at all possible. Most Christian students find it difficult to leave a highly homogenous fellowship of their peers on campus. They are uneasy and insecure with those who are chronologically below and above them. A broader span of people, however, more truly represents the church of Jesus Christ than does their campus group with an age span of only four to six years.

"I tried it, but I get tired of hearing every week about their problems with children." If you have said or felt this, let it be a challenge to learn how to introduce other topics tactfully and relevantly. Let it be a challenge to learn to be a sympathetic friend to older people with problems. You may not feel you can counsel them, but you can listen and ask questions. You might just learn something more about life. You will be working with many such people hereafter. Do not retreat to the security of your peer group.

Training

About two years passed between the time Jesus chose the apostles and when he finally sent them into the world. Earlier I discussed the intense training he gave them in that crucial interim.[4] Jesus exposed them to all kinds of life situations and taught them on the basis of their reactions to those situations. He always used concrete illustrations, whether it was the immediate event or vivid familiar imagery. He solicited opinions, urged questions, provoked harder thinking and often left discussions open-ended. He never gave up, no matter how obtuse his students were. How I wish I could teach and train as skillfully and personally as he!

We need that kind of training from someone whose life and ministry we respect. Internships have become more common in the last few years. Sometimes, however, it's more a matter of junior job assignments (to relieve the senior worker) and a written report afterward rather than some joint assignments with personal interaction and evaluation. Look, if possible, for a live-in situation with a godly discipler.

Training for missionaries comes in all shapes and circumstances. Individuals assigned to different jobs in different situations require different orientation and skills. Mission organizations (and sometimes church staffs) should be able to give you more specific counsel than could be done here. In general, the more in-depth training you get in any one or two fields, the better off you will be. Get experience in your profession. You never know how useful this is going to be in the future. Moreover, missionaries who have worked outside of Christian ministry are usually more socially mature. They seem to have a certain ballast in their lives. The person who has had only a church and Bible school social environment tends to be uncomfortable person-to-person with non-Christians (and even with other kinds of Christians) both at home and abroad.

Consider your personal enrichment and development of broader sensitivities. If you haven't begun yet, form reading habits in good literature and weekly news magazines. Join a discussion group where current events are analyzed objectively. Study the social sciences for understanding people and their cultures better, to say nothing of yourself and your cultural heritage. This especially applied to me because my parents were immigrants, and Hawaii itself is highly cosmopolitan. I needed to be clearer about my bicultural heritage. Many Americans whose forebears came to the United States earlier than mine do not know their cultural roots.

A solid Bible and theological foundation is absolutely necessary. How much formal training you need in this depends on (1) the kind of work you believe God is leading you to and (2) your religious background. In my case, my family was pagan as I grew up. After I became a Christian, I heard from the church pulpit truly inspiring stories but no systematic Bible teaching. I knew what I needed and went for it. It gave me a strong framework for developing Christian thinking. And as it turned out, it was the basis for the Bible-study ministry God called me to.

But there are other kinds of preparation. Long before I became a Christian, God was training me through the practical realities of growing up. Being a child of the Depression years prepared me for eating anything placed before me (well, almost), and for sleeping on all kinds of strange beds in unfamiliar places. And having immigrant parents meant I was brought up in two cultures with much bewilderment and clashes. This, I later realized, has helped me to understand the present university students in the Third World. For they too are usually caught between their parents' rich, centuries-old traditions and modern trends heavily influenced by Western values.

The most honing training of all was growing up with six sisters and two brothers. Each of us was as fiercely independent and energetic as our overworked parents allowed us to be. We had lots of fights and lots of fun. We learned in hard ways not merely how to get along with one another, but eventually how to respect individuality and to draw out each other's good qualities and abilities. That was the grace of God, the pure grace of God.

And to think that I sometimes resented all of these situations as I was growing up! In God's economy nothing is wasted. I can look back and see many other seemingly negative experiences that God has taken and made into positive factors for growth. I suppose that's part of what is called sanctification. I'm sure every child of God has them in his life. See how many you can find in yours.

Beginning to Serve at Home

Some years ago in Southeast Asia I was getting ready to go to the United States for a short visit. I asked some national coworkers somewhat in humor but with serious intent, "Do you have any message for our sister American churches about more missionaries?" Several clearly said they could use more help—especially in skilled, systematic teaching and applying Scripture. But two leaders in different countries said in essence the same thing. "We need more help, but we don't want inexperienced new missionaries practicing on us." Yes, experience in ministry is a big area of preparation. We all need serious hands-on experience in practical service before going to another culture to serve. I mean serious Christian service, not merely singing in the choir.

Teaching Sunday school creatively and lovingly, going beyond the published curriculum is a good starter. Leading a small house-group or evangelistic Bible study on campus may be a greater challenge, because it needs more of your continuing initiative. Some churches deliberately keep slots open on their committees for young people. If your church does not, why not suggest it? Most of us do not appreciate church administration and how hard lay leaders have to work to make it effective. Yet this kind of experience is what you may need on the field.

How about volunteering several hours a week to help your pastor on miscellaneous jobs or to research and document his sermons and writings? Such service—and there are dozens of others around the church—fosters closer fellowship with the older and (usually) wiser church members with whom we often feel an uneasy generation gap.

And please, please greet newcomers to your fellowship. Befriend them. Do not make excuses. It grieves me in "friendly" churches to see members warm and effusive with the same friends Sunday after Sunday while shy people stand around by themselves.

But don't get so involved in church activities that you have no time for service and evangelism in the community. That is spiritually fatal. After attending an urban ministries conference, one young woman excitedly testified that she had not known that one could serve God as significantly at home as across the waters. Aileen did not think, however, that Honolulu had as many needs as San Francisco. That may be so. But to her surprise, a church staff member immediately ticked off a list of six community service agencies using their own church facilities. He pointed out that they were still looking for more volunteer help, and in some cases salaried staff, whom they would gladly train to help abused children, child abusers, culturally deprived children and so on.

Within a one- to three-mile radius she could join other church members already involved in ministries of compassion—feeding and clothing the poor in the nearby housing project, conducting worship services and spending time with the lonely at the nursing home, leading group Bible studies at the prison, playing with retarded children at the state home, running evangelistic activities at the detention home for juvenile delinquents. Aileen was amazed there were so many needs right around her.

Gifts and Servants

"Yes, but I don't have the gift for that." This is often a cop-out for some Christians when certain obvious needs arise. Sometimes I am asked by young Christians how they can discover their gifts. I have to answer them in the only practical way I know: Don't worry about your gifts. You will never know what they are until you start serving God by serving others. Keep your eyes and your heart open. Who needs help? How can you help? Do what you can in the best way possible. Then one day it will dawn on you what the Spirit has especially gifted you with to build up that part of the church. By then you will not be worrying about gifts. You will be too busy serving.

Lopsided teaching about and the abuse of gifts have caused unnecessary tensions as well as inferiority and superiority complexes. We sometimes seem to be back in the confusion of Corinth (1 Cor 12 and 14). I usually prefer to use the word *contributions* instead of *gifts*. For instance, "One of Marion's contributions to the fellowship is her compassion." Or, "Earl contributes to the body by his occasional but wise counsel."

Being overly concerned about one's gifts leads to unhealthy self-consciousness. Jesus says nothing about gifts in the Pauline sense. But he certainly has a lot to say about serving others. To serve one another, or rather as Jesus put it, *to be* servants to one another—this was the hardest lesson for the Twelve. Their appointment as Jesus' apostles gave them heady ideas about prestige and power. Jesus had to use a startling analogy to teach them what true greatness is. "Whoever wants to become great among you must be your servant *[diakonos]*, and whoever wants to be first must be slave *[doulos]* of all" (Mk 10:43-44).

I don't think that the servant-slave analogy hits North American Christians as hard as it hit those Jewish disciples. Many house servants in the West get good pay and go home after a day's work. Likewise for janitors and garbage collectors, who often earn more than teachers, though their jobs still carry some stigma. Here servants can vote; there slaves had no civil rights. Slaves were their master's property for him to do with as he willed. Jesus' comparison was radical to the ears of the Twelve. He was training them to identify with the despised and oppressed of their society.

A good servant does not simply obey his master's explicit commands. He anticipates his master's implicit wish and looks around to see what needs to be done not only for his master but for his fellow servants. This is what pleases the Master.

Crossing Cultural Barriers at Home

Lastly, it is absolutely essential for missionary candidates to involve themselves in crosscultural ministries while still at home. We need not pass national borders to cross cultural boundaries. We cross a social frontier when we go to the other side of town where poor people live to tell them about Jesus and show his love for them in practical ways. We cross a racial barrier on our campus when we pass over to the other side of the cafeteria to have lunch with foreign students or with local students of another ethnic group. We cross an educational frontier when we walk over to the other side of the living room to talk with our parents who have had less education than ourselves.

North American Christians can never say they have little opportunity for crosscultural service at home. Compared to other countries, Canada and the United States have doors wide open to immigrants. Their universities and colleges are temporary homes for tens of thousands of overseas students. Christian students at the University of Hawaii play volleyball (an international game) with overseas students each week. Some tutor Laotian and Vietnamese refugees in English. Some take them to the supermarket and teach them how to shop—without bargaining. The president of their chapter is crossing another kind of cultural barrier as he tutors prison inmates in math. He says his greatest crosscultural trial is to remember to wear shoes on the highly polished prison floors rather than his customary Japanese slippers. He also has begun an evening Bible teaching service at a Chinese Episcopal church. Opportunities are at every turn.

No, the world is not only way out there somewhere. It is right at our doorstep, across the street, in city hall, at the high school. We must know the world in our own community before going overseas. We must exercise a crosscultural ministry at home, for we are not likely to do so all of a sudden when we get overseas. We are more likely to slip into a missionary subculture with colleagues of like mind.

A missionary with a subcultural mentality probably began developing it at home. A Latin American Christian I know used to be disturbed that so many missionaries could not participate in the Spanish culture—community festivities, arts, literature, music and so on. Then he went north to study. He discovered that the kind of churches they came from encouraged living in a subculture. Back home these missionaries participated only in their church life. They had practically nothing to do with the life in their community or with broader cultural interests in general. In other words, whether in North or South America they were living in subcultures. They had problems in crossing cultural barriers south of the border because they had never learned to cross cultural barriers at home. Yet the Lord Jesus who saved them sought to cross every foreign barrier in his own small community for love's sake.

Following Jesus across these near frontiers is part of being a disciple and prepares one to make disciples anywhere. A well-loved missionary I worked with in Indonesia used to intrigue me with her earlier experiences in the Appalachians of West Virginia. Clearly her service there had been invaluable training in making her culturally sensitive and compassionate. Comparing her two major crosscultural experiences, she said the first was the more severe trial that she nearly failed. "But," she observed, "it prepared me for an easier adjustment to Indonesians and their culture."

7

MAKING DISCIPLES IN OTHER CULTURES

IN 1955 WHEN I WAS ASKED to join the IVCF-USA staff, my first and sincere response was, "Oh, good night, no! I'm not the intellectual type. I can't answer all the students' questions about science and the Bible, existentialism and all that." How grateful I am for the clear, crisp answer I received. "We are not asking you to intellectualize Christianity. We are asking you to join us in teaching and sharing with students all that you know about living and working with Jesus Christ."

With that one statement came two points that sped me along the road of Christian service. The first was the focus on the heart of our mission: making disciples. The second was the emphasis on teamwork: "*We* are asking you to join *us*." A third point gradually dawned on me: The university world is a world of its own with a proud culture, and a rich heritage. But it is a culture hostile to the gospel. Right there my first crosscultural ministry began.

Teaching and sharing with others all that we know about living and working with Jesus Christ—when we take this in dead seriousness we are making disciples. Next to his work of redemption Jesus' most important work was making disciples. How clearly we see this priority directly affects our ministry.

Jesus, Our Model

Jesus did not simply preach and teach great messages. He did not make mere converts. Arguing with the scribes and Pharisees was not his main occupation. Not even healing and casting out demons were his highest goals. Yes, he fed thousands. He attracted hundreds of disciples. He even sent out seventy-two of them for a special evangelistic assignment. But he called only twelve men to be his constant companions, to whom he gave special training. He occasionally concentrated on three or only one for even more specialized training.

In less than three years, he had so trained the Twelve that he could turn over his work to them permanently. He had left them a foundation and a pattern for leadership in reaching other people. His trust in them was well grounded, for his work has lasted to this day.

The heart of our mission has two distinct but inseparable sides, to make disciples (chapters seven and eight) and to grow disciple makers (chapters eleven and twelve). We are to make disciples in such a way that they will be able to make disciples who will be able to make disciples who will be able to. . . . This is the intent and spirit of Paul's last repeated instruction to Timothy, his younger coworker. "And the things you have heard me say in the presence of many witnesses entrust to reliable men who will also be qualified to teach others" (2 Tim 2:2).

We need not guess or grope in the dark about how to make disciples and grow disciple makers. Jesus has left us his own superb example. So have Paul and the other apostles. The four Gospels comprise the best manual on the subject. Acts and the letters to young churches reinforce this. Why do we look for short cuts? There are none. Why do we slavishly try to follow the formula of some human authority? We should learn from the insights of others but always return to the New Testament.

"He shared his spirit till they caught his vision." The unknown believer who said this had himself caught Jesus' spirit and vision. This was one of Jesus' major "methods" of training his apostles. It pervaded everything he did in his training of the Twelve. To what extent can we follow Jesus in training disciples?[5]

It has always bothered me that we who are supposed to be training disciples have only minimal time with them—a few hours a week at most. In some countries we have developed two-, three- or four-week leadership training courses for the students. But none can begin to compare with Jesus' twenty-four-hours-a-day, seven-days-a-week exposure to his disciples. This would not be possible in most situations, so we say. The Discipleship Training Center in Singapore and the Asian Bible Center in India have been established to try to get closer to Jesus' model.[6]

The discipleship training that Operation Mobilization (OM) offers its young recruits is the demanding kind that many young people are looking for today. It is a short-term on-the-job training which can help participants learn more about themselves and their capacities for further frontline missionary work. Much of their literature distribution work on land is in Europe, the Middle East and India. Their two ships, *Doulos* and *Logos,* go to other continents. They draw young people from all over the world for a summer, or a year or two. They work with experienced leaders in bold ways. They dare to go where God shows. The disciplines they strictly enforce, especially between the sexes, would discourage many an American Christian used to a more permissive society, for they run a tight ship on board and on land. But many workers are witnesses to the fact that they learned more about real discipleship during one year on an Operation Mobilization ship than they had in all their previous years of being a Christian.

If I were at least half my present age (and knew what I now know about working overseas), I would do what Ann from the University of Richmond did. As an active member of her campus Christian fellowship she had been stirred to participate directly in God's global mission. Her major in French opened the door for a Fulbright scholarship on French-African literature at the University of Yaoundé.

When I met her at the regional student congress, she gave me a warm welcome. The first thing I noticed was how pale she was—white, not even pink. Her African cotton dress hung loosely on her slight figure. Then I noticed that her white legs were full of red insect bites. I remember my inward reaction of "Hurray for her for not being overly concerned with comfort and appearance." But I also wondered, What kind of creature is this? Why isn't she living in more comfortable quarters off campus where she could eat better and be free of the insects? I soon found out.

She had arrived a year earlier and immediately sought out the Christian fellowship on campus. It was then experiencing some growing pains. She quickly recognized who the real leaders were and knew that even with her limited experience that she could help prepare guides and train Bible study leaders. There was no question about living off campus in better quarters. Living in the residential hall with other women students, she had maximum time with the people she had come to serve. That first year so many more Bible study groups formed that the administration called her in for a warning and ordered the groups off campus. But the work kept growing.

Ann is quick to point to the solid foundation laid down by her African coworkers and missionary predecessors, and she is the first to admit the mistakes and unwise things she did along the way before she finally left the student work in the hands of local leaders after about three years. But what is significant about her contribution at that stage of growth in the work was that she was willing to live, study, work and play with those on campus twenty-four hours a day during those years.

Identification—How Far?

Jesus is our model not only in how to make disciples but also in attitudes and relationship to people. To reach us Jesus had to become one of us. In his Incarnation—stupendous event!— he totally identified with us in our humanity. It was not a pretense at being human, as Hindu legends openly state about their gods who came as "men" to earth. "Since the children have flesh and blood, he too shared in their humanity so that by his death he might destroy him who holds the power of death—that is, the devil" (Heb 2:14). What then does it mean for missionaries today to identify with the people they want to reach?

Father Joseph Damien (1840-1889) followed Jesus' example to an inspiring extreme. He was a young Roman Catholic priest who left Belgium to minister to the lepers on the island of Molokai (Hawaii). God gave him a deep compassion for these pitiable outcasts of society. In letters to his family and friends, he spoke of his flock as "my brothers and sisters."

As he lived with them and lovingly ministered to their spiritual and physical needs, he too became a leper. Thereafter in his letters he would say, without regret, "we lepers." How far should a missionary identify with a people's culture and living situation? As far as Father Damien? The answer, I believe, is as far as we can in order to communicate Jesus Christ clearly.

For their field work, two seminary students rented an apartment among the Blacks and Hispanics in New York City, and quietly assumed their lifestyle. Their work eventually bore fruit. But at the end, they said they could never totally identify with the people they had come to love. The reason was that they could move out of that wretched neighborhood anytime they wanted to. The others could not. The two students concluded honestly that not identification but participation in the lives and struggles of the people was the key.

People do not expect us to be exactly like them. The attempt to do so can be artificial or patronizing. They want us to be our authentic selves, but with a genuine respect for them, their ways of living and their cultural values. They love it when we naturally participate in their family and community life. They are delighted when we know their literature and try to learn more about their unique arts and crafts.

Ao Dais Are Not for Buffaloes

Sometimes identification merely in outward things can be ridiculous. I recall some students at a church social in Saigon giggling at the sight of some large missionaries wearing the *ao dai*. The *ao dai* is extremely graceful, and it is no wonder that the willowy Vietnamese women have always preferred it to Western dresses. But it is also very formfitting. My language tutor whispered to me, "It is better for these missionaries to wear their own clothes. In the *ao dai* they look like water buffaloes." Then and there I knew that I would never wear the *ao dai* unless I had some indication that it was acceptable to their national taste.

The Indian *sari* is equally graceful, but that was not my problem. When Chandapilla, the director of the student work in India, invited me to work with his staff, he stipulated that I lower my skirts. In those days of Mary Quant's miniskirts, I thought that my one-inch above the knees was very conservative among the girls I was working with then in Southeast Asia. By the time I got to India two years later, maxis were having their brief fling in fashion. On the first evening after my arrival in Madras, I happened to be wearing one that I had just been given in Pakistan. It was in vogue—high-necked, long-sleeved, ankle-length. Chanda appeared at the door in his rough cotton *dhoti* and *kurta*. I could not resist. "Well, brother Chanda," I asked, "how am I doing with this missionary dress?" He promptly answered, "Sister Ada, I personally do not care what kind of clothes you wear. But I want our women to be comfortable with you." That is still the best advice in *any* country.

Food, Burps and Slurps

Food is often an obvious clue to our adjustments because it is so important to everybody in everyday living. We grow up with emotional attachments to certain foods. It may not be necessary to eat native food three times a day with the acceptable slurps and burps. But not to eat any at all except in their homes on special occasions speaks loudly of proud refusal to participate in their common life. To wince at their burps and slurps is plain rudeness.

Picnics were special to us as teen-agers. No matter what race we were everyone took Japanese *musubi* (rice balls wrapped in seaweed) and the *okazu* that go along with them. These could be readily bought at shops if not made at home. One day a missionary family came with us. As we opened our lunches, all could see that theirs was conspiciously different. One of the young people muttered in disgust under his breath, "Five years in Hawaii and still bringing sandwiches and doughnuts to picnics!"

Many new dishes are easy to take because they are not too strange. One can recognize familiar ingredients, though in different combinations and with different seasoning. Other new dishes are recognizable but still strange. It was dinnertime when I arrived in Yaoundé on my first visit to French-speaking Africa. My Swiss missionary hosts and our African colleague suggested that we go directly from the airport to "the best restaurant in town." My first thought was that Claude and Anne-Marie, like many missionaries, had a favorite European restaurant for special occasions. Perhaps French? Oo la la! No, it was a local restaurant— plain, neat, clean. But I was not quite sure what to make of the menu. Isaac, our colleague, was helpful: "The three best choices are monkey, antelope and porcupine." Claude and Anne-Marie ate their monkey meat with genuine relish. I made it through the antelope meat by the grace of God.

A few principles have helped me when confronted with strange new dishes. (1) Common sense: If millions of people here have survived on this food, why shouldn't I? (2) Love: If my friends enjoy this food, why can't I? (3) A paraphrase of 1 Corinthians 10:25: Eat everything that is placed before you, asking no questions. (4) Commitment: Where he leads me, I will follow; what he feeds me, I will swallow. (5) Prayer: Lord, I'll take it in. You keep it in.

Compounditis and a Servant's Room

Before I went overseas the one missionary disease I commonly heard about was compounditis. This has been particularly true of prewar missionaries and certain affluent denominational missions. Later, I saw for myself the infected missionaries seemingly quarantined in their Western-style homes behind their high, whitewashed walls.

It is not fair to think of all missionaries as so diseased. For there are others who live as simply as the Lord Jesus did. They maintain only the necessities of a lifestyle that enhance their service while enjoying, as their Lord did, the larger home of God's community. That is sensible. For is it not bizarre for missionaries to live far above the level of the people to whom they are servants?

I learned much about missionary identification (that I had only known in theory before) from an unusual source. It was during the toughest assignment I have had—so far—in a country where the work had not got off the ground even after seven or eight years. God then raised up another one that took off dramatically in one or two years. I was sent there to work for unity between the two organizations. Alas, I was no Mary Slessor, the once-timid Scottish lass who successfully mediated between two warring tribes in Africa and opened the way to greater evangelization. I have never felt more frustrated. I have never wept more. I have never been angrier with God.

But God gave me a sheltering vine, as he had for angry Jonah. The missionary (from the deep south) whom he used to start the second movement helped to preserve my sanity. Sarah also taught me how to truly identify with people. She never said a word, but her example was powerful. A few years earlier, she had been the first in her denominational mission to leap over their compound walls. Her radical move to rent a local house in town probably embarrassed some of her fellow missionaries. By the time I came along, the house had been turned into a student center. Sarah's personal space was the tiny servant's room between the kitchen and the large meeting room. The room was big enough, literally, for three bodies lying down. How do I know this precise measurement? If I visited her overnight, that was where I slept—on the mat with her and her national coworker.

Hananim and Shang Tai

South Korea is one of the two countries often cited for phenomenal church growth; Brazil is the other. The Christian population has been growing faster than the national population. This openness to Christianity has been in South Korea since the first Presbyterian missionaries arrived one hundred years ago. Many books and articles have been written on this phenomenon and its causes.

One such book, S. J. Palmer's *Korea and Christianity*[1] makes an interesting comparison between missionary work in Korea and in China. Palmer's thesis is that the Korea missionaries were more effective on a national scale because they took seriously the basic religious concepts and other traditions they found in Korean culture. They built on these, showing the people that Jesus Christ is the full and final revelation of their *Hananim* (the one true God).

On the other hand, Palmer cites cases of missionaries to China who rejected out of hand the Chinese *Shang Tai* (the God above) and the cultural traditions that were abhorrent to their own cultural senses. They considered them purely heathen concepts and practice. No doubt some were indeed pagan, as I know from some of my mother's leftover practices in my childhood in Hawaii. For instance, she used to move our little fevered bodies over a pan of fire while she chanted prayers of healing to the spirits.

It is only fair to point out that there have been missionaries to China who were culturally sensitive and respectful. In Hong Kong and Macao, one can find schools and colleges named after a highly respected missionary, Matteo Ricci (1552-1611). He was born into a noble Italian family. He was probably the man most responsible for gaining a permanent foothold for Christianity in China. His aristocratic background no doubt was admirably suited for establishing good rapport with Chinese scholars and government officials during his ten years in Peking.

But Ricci had more than his family background to commend him. He was a scientist who had advanced knowledge of mathematics, astronomy and geography, which he shared with his hosts. This opened doors that other Christian missionaries had been unable to go through. As soon as he entered China, he studied the Chinese culture, philosophies and traditions. He learned the language well. He even assumed the dress of a Confucian scholar. He respected the people and accepted them as they were; they accepted him and listened to him. The records show that many high-ranking people professed faith in Jesus Christ.

It is also only fair to remember that the early China missionaries faced a vaster expanse of land and a people who had a more conquering nature than those that the Korea missionaries faced. The nineteenth-century missionaries were children of their times. They were born in a small world and weaned on national pride— the sun never set on the British Empire, which God (they believed) had singularly blessed for his glory. How else could they have responded? This is not to excuse their national chauvinism, but to remember that we are all children of our times. The British national sentiment of the nineteenth and early twentieth centuries seems to be resounding with an American accent in the media of the late twentieth century.

The thesis of Palmer, however, is still worth more detailed consideration to see how valid his analysis is. In 1981, Don Richardson applied it to other cultures in his book *Eternity in Their Hearts*. He describes the kind of discoveries that missionaries and anthropologists have made in non-Christian cultures, where remnants of the revelation of God can be found. Like Palmer, he brings attention to the importance of understanding and respecting the culture of the people to whom God sends us.

To reject a people's cultural forms, to despise their customs even though they may be religiously neutral, to throw out their religious beliefs without much examination—is this not communicating our lack of respect for the people themselves?

The Unknown God

Palmer's illustration about *Shang Tai* made me think about the ways my sisters and I had tried to explain the gospel to our parents. We had tried many different ways, but with no positive response from them. Conditioned by certain evangelical convictions, we had thought that unless our words were a literal "preaching of Christ crucified and him only," it was unbiblical, weak, compromising. Like some of those early missionaries to China, we had also thought that all religious beliefs of other cultures were totally outside of God's revelation and grace. To include *Shang Tai* in our witness would lead only to some kind of syncretism.

God graciously gave me another opportunity years later when I was home with our parents again. The door squeaked open for me to study the Gospel of John with them. (For cultural and psychological reasons I studied with each separately.) What a difference it made that my attitude was respectful of what faith they did have! It was natural for us to talk about *Shang Tai*. In her seventies, Mother came to a clear faith in Jesus Christ. Father was never as clear as Mother, but I had to leave that with God. God had indeed used many witnesses through the years to lead up to this. But I have no doubt that a turning point was when I became a more sensitive and sensible evangelist.

I should have known this earlier from Paul the Apostle. For this is precisely what he did in Athens. He began with their belief in a Creator and their admission of the need to worship "The Unknown God," and led them up to the resurrection (Acts 17:22-32). Some evangelicals, however, interpret the fact that he was laughed out of town as evidence that he had used the wrong evangelistic approach, for he "never once mentions the name of Jesus." That was, of course, because he was interrupted in his sermon. Paul used this same approach in evangelizing the less sophisticated pagans in Lystra with rather different results (Acts 14:8-18).

Nonwhite Mistakes

Surely, we should learn all we can from both good and bad examples. For a while I used to hear an occasional new missionary criticize the "prewar missionaries" or "old China hands" with a scarcely hidden superiority. I can quickly recognize it because of my own earlier struggles. When I first went overseas, though ten years older than the average new missionary (and supposedly wiser), I secretly felt the same superiority. I had read and heard enough about those imperialistic white missionaries. I had even met some, so I was determined that I would never make their white mistakes. I did not. I made my own nonwhite mistakes.

A hard but essential lesson to learn is that *different* does not necessarily mean *inferior* or *wrong*. We tend to make value judgments about other people's cultural forms and activities when we feel strange or threatened. Before I became a Christian, and though I am Chinese, I used to laugh at the Cantonese opera. I thought that ridiculous show should have died with the Ming dynasty (or with whichever dynasty it originated). To me it was noisy and meaningless. The highly stylized motions seemed comical. As kids, for sheer fun, we used to imitate the high, nasal pentatonic singing.

Years later in Singapore, for my cultural orientation a friend suggested a Cantonese opera going on below in the street. I gulped and wanted to tell her I knew all about it, thank you. But of course I went. She explained the symbols of the props, each costume, each motion. I learned how many of the stories conveyed a rich history and such treasured social values as sacrificial courage, filial piety, loyalty to the emperor and so on. Suddenly there was meaning in what had been empty before.

I had to adapt to different forms of Christian worship. The first time I was in a prayer meeting in Korea, I was horrified to hear seventy-five people praying aloud and calling on the Lord at the same time. And these were Presbyterians! To me it was highly irreverent. Then the leader pounded on the pulpit. Instantly there was perfect silence. To me it was authoritarian. A brother who had been abroad must have noted my apparently visible reaction. In kindness he remarked, "Your churches are quieter, aren't they? I think that's why so many fall asleep during the sermon."

If a missionary is basically a servant of the Lord Jesus, many common problems are eliminated or at least more readily worked out. Then we may have God's grace to cross those invisible but rugged mountain frontiers of racial feelings, cultural strangeness, climate and diet changes. To shift mental and emotional gears to a different pace of life, so we are not always looking at our watches and tapping our feet. To adjust to a different standard of living with varying ideas of hygiene and sanitation so we become less neurotic about our health. To empathize with people in their personal dilemmas so we do not always have to analyze but can weep with those who weep. To communicate Jesus Christ so that he makes sense to needy men and women in their situations. To persist in the face of inevitable opposition from the devil. These are impossible without the heart of a servant.

8

MAKING DISCIPLES ACROSS BARRIERS

TELL US ABOUT YOUR funny experiences in learning the language and making cultural mistakes." I can expect this request when I am asked to speak on missions. It's easy to entertain with humorous, exotic stories. It's harder to talk about the barriers facing those who would disciple the nations. In the last chapter we discussed the visible and obvious cultural differences missionaries face. In this chapter we will consider barriers that are less obvious. Some we raise ourselves, others are an inherent part of the international challenge of missions today.

Some Personal Barriers
Americans, for example, do not like to be considered provincial, especially in Europe. We vehemently reject the image of the

country bumpkin coming into town still smelling of the fields. Yet many of us feel like this when visiting or living in cultures older and richer than ours. We are not more provincial than many other national groups, but we are often more conspicuous because our limited views are more loudly and repeatedly expressed. This sometimes happens in speaking English to a foreigner. If he does not respond immediately and we think that he has not understood, we repeat the sentence more slowly and with increasing volume.

We have put high premiums on certain values like individuality, creativity, forthrightness, friendliness, a sense of adventure, self-assertion and so on. Unfortunately, in an immature person these often come off as individualism, eccentricity, insensitivity, superficiality, instability or abrasiveness. Even if we are not consciously proud of these values, our own cultural conditioning sets us up for a clash with societies where these qualities are not as prominent (but still present) as others which they prize more highly.

A seminary intern I met in the United States once spent six months with a student movement. I had seen his excellent qualities while in his campus fellowship. So when his seminary professor had sent me a form of endorsement, I had given a positive reply. At the end of his stint, his local supervisor gave me an oral evaluation of the intern's work and relationship with the university students. By the time he finished, I was red in the face, both for the young intern and for myself for endorsing him. As far as this national supervisor was concerned (and he was a kindly person), all the intern's good qualities and good preparations went down the drain because of his condescending attitudes. He had expressed his chauvinistic nationalism and had lost whatever credibility he had come with. I had not observed these attitudes when I first met him in the United States. But with the students in this new culture he constantly extolled the American virtue of "being an individual in your own right." Then, further frustrated because the students would not work on his bright ideas, he began scolding them for not taking individual initiative more quickly.

In theory, he understood that these young people came from a culture with strong family and clan ties. Yet he could not accept their value of quiet, intuitive group consensus—which takes more time to achieve. He "knew" but could not accept the reality that one cannot and does not have to toss out these and other cultural values when one is converted to Christ. He wanted eighty people to conform to his cultural values rather than try to work with them in their community values.

When I talked with the young man himself, I felt for him. All he could splutter was, "Yes, but. . . . Yes, but. . . . Yes, but. . . ." He did not see himself as others saw him until two years afterward. We bumped into each other at a conference. He had learned from that painful experience and matured mightily.

The overfamiliar way that some American Christians approach God or talk about him is appalling to people of other cultures. A Filipino engineer struggled a long time before he became a Christian because of this stumbling block. Like eighty-five per cent of the Philippine population, he came from a Roman Catholic background. He had attended an evangelistic meeting. As he listened he became fascinated with "the Protestant religion." But when he heard the missionary evangelist pray after the message, he was shocked by the tone of voice. He considered it disrespectful, a tone of equality with God. He wondered what kind of physical posture Protestants assumed in praying. So he opened his eyes. This was even worse. "There he was in his plaid trousers. His legs were apart, and his hands were on his hips, just like a father showing his authority to children."

Cultural Cues and Social Skills
Respect and thoughtfulness of others should be basic in our discipleship. When I first heard the phrase *social skills,* it sounded strange, as *methods, personnel, programmed, recycle, function* and *relational* do to most non-North Americans. What a relief it was to realize that people were talking about old-fashioned good manners, common courtesy, graciousness or what some call love.

Whichever term one chooses to use, this quality seems to be lacking in some of us when we go overseas. The lack is revealed both in our acts and in our words. In several countries in Asia, it is customary to take off one's shoes before entering a house. This is for physical cleanliness and for the philosophical reason of leaving the world behind as one enters the sanctuary of a home. Naturally nothing is said by the hosts, though some have house slippers available at the door. This custom is so obvious that it is difficult to imagine how some people can walk into a dustless house with dusty shoes on. Yet I have heard some mutter as they left their shoes on, "Oh, they don't expect foreigners to do it." Or, "My shoes aren't that dirty." Or, "I've got holes in my socks." Just as insensitive is the guest who never even realizes that everybody else is padding around shoeless! Most foreigners, however, learn early in their orientation about such obvious customs. And not even the rudest of us would enter such a house with shoes on more than once. We at least remember the next time to wear new socks.

When we are suddenly confronted with many strange things at the very time that we want to prove our usefulness, it is a natural reflex to revert to our own cultural patterns. We can get in our own way with a careless tongue. "At home we," "I," "me," "mine," "In the U.S./England/Canada we," "Why don't you people," "As far as *I'm* concerned, *I'd* like for us to," come tumbling out with alarming frequency. These slips of the lip reveal a we-they attitude which "they" clearly recognize. Such words emphasize rather than minimize our differences. If this attitude remains unchecked, it spells the demise of missionary service for that person. The cultural umbilical cord has not yet been cut. Unless it is, there can be no independent life in the new culture.

I am not advocating the death of our own cultural identity. That is neither desirable nor possible. In the heyday of the hippie culture we learned in a frightening way that when young people tried to disown their despised cultural identity, they became nonpersons. No, cultural identity is the basic warp and woof of personal identity. But the ultimate pattern of our lives will be richly enhanced when we are able to weave in color and designs from other cultures. J. Hudson Taylor used to counsel the new missionaries that went overseas with the China Inland Mission (now Overseas Missionary Fellowship), "Eliminate the unnecessary. Minimize the differences." May I add, "Capitalize on the similarities."

Common courtesy or social skills derive basically from being thoughtful of others. It takes time to observe and reflect on why people respond or do not respond in a certain way, and how we ourselves may have heard or communicated something quite different from what was intended. One guideline is *consciously* to work hard at what we know is right. That will help offset the social gaffes that we are all bound to commit unconsciously. People understand and forgive when they see that we are trying hard. In fact, these gaffes might be the topic of amused, sympathetic conversation in the neighborhood for days afterward. And if you are humble enough to ask for help, they usually are delighted to give help. They feel honored that you respect their way of life and care enough to ask. Isn't that love?

Sometimes misunderstandings occur when many of the local people speak English as their second or third language, as would be true in the Philippines or former British colonies on all continents. We are likely to assume that since they speak the same language we do, they also mean the same thing or feel the same emotion associated with certain words or ideas. As Churchill once said, Americans and the British are people divided by a common language. We must be alert to nuances and connotations that may be completely different from what we expect.

In a central Asian country a local leader (not the pastor) once said to me, "I want you to speak in our church on Sunday." What an honor to speak at the largest church in town! We discussed what kind of message would be helpful for that congregation. As it was already Saturday, I stayed up late that night to prepare. The next morning I sat in the front row with our brother, waiting to bring God's Word to the people. I never did. He never said a word, nor did he seem the least bit perturbed. Rather, he was praising God for the message that the pastor had brought. On reflection, I realized that he had meant something else: How I wish you could speak at our church one of these Sundays; but under the circumstances that is not possible.

That was not the end. Some time later in a neighboring town another local leader said to me, "I want you to speak in our church on Sunday." This time I was prepared not to prepare a special message. I forgot about it, and on the following Sunday accompanied my friends to church. I was introduced and assumed it was the customary welcome to guests. Then while I was still standing in the pew, the pastor said with beaming face, "Now our sister will bring us the morning message that God has given to her, and Brother Ezra will be her translator." Well! God had to give me a message as I walked to the pulpit.

Learning to discern and interpret or reinterpret cultural cues is nothing mysterious. But it does demand observation and polite questioning. One American businessman used to be frustrated in the Philippines when a repairman would not appear at the appointed time. He concluded that they were lying and undependable when they said on the phone, yes, they would come. Then someone gave him a tip, and by his own survey he learned that if the other person hesitated for about six seconds before saying yes, he was really saying, "No, I'm sorry I can't come." He learned further to reinterpret the nonverbal communication as, "I don't want either one of us to lose face by a direct refusal."

Being culturally sensitive and thoughtful of others does not begin after one passes through immigration. Or even in missionary orientation. It began long ago in the formation of our characters. It is amazing to hear people claim to be experienced in crosscultural relationships because they have lived briefly in one or even two different cultures and yet to observe their insensitivity to others at home. Some of my colleagues who have worked longer than I in different cultures are the first to say that they have to start from scratch in every new society they enter, including their own home base which keeps changing in constituency and cultural values. They are growing people, fully alive and alert to others as fellow human beings.

I wish I had been as humble as they when I went to my fourth Asian country. With hindsight I now can see more clearly what happened. I thought I understood all Asians, having lived and worked closely with Asians in three other countries and being Asian myself. Moreover, I was used to this same racial group in Hawaii. But in this fourth country, I botched it culturally. At times I did not know who I was more upset with—the nationals, God or myself. But those years, humiliating with failure as they were, proved to be the cleansing I needed for greater responsibilities the Lord was preparing me for.

Witnessing Up
Some barriers are subtle and unexpected. Years ago Dr. W. Dayton Roberts of Latin American Mission challenged Christians to "witness up"—to reach the upper social classes. He illustrated his appeal with the many opportunities he was having for Bible study groups in Latin American homes. That challenge spread. Today it has become more common for missionary organizations to assign people to work among the upper classes.

Last year a Peruvian colleague, Samuel Escobar, organized a training course that included not only the expected students but professional people from these upper social classes. Samuel is more at home with them than I. But since I had to do most of the teaching, I was nervous. My apprehensions were compounded when I saw on the list of participants some aristocratic Castillian names. I was sure I would be culturally gauche. I was. I was also afraid that when it came time to divide into small discussion groups people would feel socially awkward. They did not. For two weeks they sat naturally alongside the less well-dressed young people. They participated as eagerly and humbly as the expectedly enthusiastic students.

This witnessing up, of course, is not new. Jesus was always doing it. So was Paul. Others have done it since then. In some cases, like Matteo Ricci, they were not witnessing up, but alongside. The practice of many missionary organizations in the past has been to go to the lower social classes. On the subcontinent of India, Pakistan and Bangladesh, many of the first Christians were from the "sweeper" caste, just as many of the first Corinthian Christians were from the slave or lower classes (1 Cor 1:26). It was logical, as they were the responsive ones. We ourselves tend to witness *down* in personal evangelism. It is psychologically easier. But upper social classes are included prominently in the "all nations" that the Lord Jesus commanded us to reach for him. They have the same needs and aspirations we do.

The Hardest Field of All
But there remain some really tough fields where the gospel has barely penetrated. The Muslim world stands out prominently as the hardest field of all. Nearly every literate Christian knows of Samuel Zwemer's witness to Christ in this impenetrable world. He labored for forty years without seeing one convert. Yet he never gave up. With other students, he organized the Arabic Mission, moving from Basrah to Bahrain to Muscat to Kuwait. Then he based himself in an interdenominational study center in Cairo. From here he continued to challenge the church to Muslim evangelism. Others considered his mission an impossible one. To the end of his life, he still considered it a glorious privilege, not a meaningless sacrifice.

With its incredible oil riches, the Arab world has become more openly militant in its Islamic faith. No Muslim ever forgets that the parallel growth of Christianity and Islam has meant centuries of mutual bloody hostilities. He sees only the injustices and slaughters committed by Christians against his people. There is no separation of mosque and state. When either is threatened, both rise up in combined malevolent power. The *kamikaze* bombings of American military buildings and French embassies may be committed by fanatics, but they symbolize the Muslim anger and hatred toward Christians.

There are, however, small pockets of Christians throughout the Muslim world. In Egypt the pocket is much bigger. In Indonesia Islam is not as militant as in the Arab world. In fact, it is mixed with native animism. Here there have been more conversions to Christianity. In Europe and North America, tens of thousands of Muslim students spend several crucial years in universities. Here they are slightly more open than they could be at home. In north Africa, Christian university lecturers, students and other tentmakers have been quietly witnessing. Recently, in one north African country, it was reported that a tiny trickle of conversions has become more visible week by week. This is a sign of hope and a reminder to us that the Muslim world is a part of the whole world that God loves.

Other Difficult Areas

Since the end of World War 2, many North Americans have gone to Europe as missionaries. Europe is a magnet. Each summer in Austria the International Fellowship of Evangelical Students has international conferences. By the end of the month, many a romantic student (and the Lord uses such) has had a vision to return as "a witness to non-Christian Europe." Often these visions have to do with climbing every mountain to the sound of music— and visiting Florentine art galleries. Such visions disappear, of course, when realities loom large.

Anglo-Saxon missionaries to Europe have adjustments rather different from those who go to countries in the Third World. In broad terms, they work in post-Christian countries rather than pre-Christian ones. They find people hardened to the message of Jesus Christ because they have known Christianity only in the form of institutionalized religion, which has some big, question-able patches in its history. Because they could not persist in such an atmosphere, many missionaries have had to leave Europe early.

For some, there is another reason, often left unsaid: they feel culturally inferior. And that hurts. They have been paralyzed in their attempts to witness up culturally.

The survivors are those who, like missionaries elsewhere, have had to work hard at cultural acceptance. Europeans can be highly articulate in their criticisms of both Britishers and Americans, especially in the summertime. So when I meet missionary survivors in Paris or Marburg or Lisbon, I find myself in awe of them, like those I know who work in Muslim areas. They seem to have a quieter air about them.

Japanese are not as vocal in their criticisms as are people in the West. They certainly have opinions, but do not express them as readily. It would be considered presumptuous. This drives Americans crazy, and makes them agree that "Japan is the hardest mission field in the world." This hyperbolic statement draws attention to the long, uphill history of missions there—from the persecutions of the earliest Roman Catholic missionaries in the late sixteenth century to the post-World War 2 years. The statistic of .05% is often quoted as the miniscule number of Christians in Japan after so many years of evangelism. Others cite the figure of .05% for Roman Catholics and 1.2% for Protestants.[8] Even this is an extremely low return for missionary labors.

Another way of expressing the difficulties of missionary work in Japan is to point out that there seem to be more personal casualties among missionaries there than elsewhere. I think the reasons may be similar to those of European missionaries who leave early. It is harder to penetrate the cultural curtain. One mission director frankly admitted to a group of us, "We have been sending a bunch of farmers to the most literate country in the world." At the same time some of the most effective missionaries I know are in Japan. Those who have faithfully persisted for ten, twenty, thirty years have begun to see a miniscule percentage of Christians rise up, however slightly.

At the feet of the majestic Himalayas lies the Hindu kingdom of Nepal, which has never allowed missionaries to come in and proselytize. But it has permitted Christian educators and medical people to come in to serve their needy people. When the doors were opened in 1951, a few veteran missionaries from India entered in such capacities. Indian Christians have been teaching in schools scattered in the mountain areas. At present about one hundred eighty workers serve through the United Mission to Nepal, a fellowship of more than thirty-two Asian and Western missions.[9] The tiny church has been growing, but not without imprisonments and other kinds of persecution. Nepal, which is north of India, is typical of many smaller countries neighboring larger, more evangelized countries. It makes sense to pray that more Christians from neighboring Asian countries will enter such countries like Nepal and Burma, where Western missionaries cannot.

Yes, there are barriers within and without—political, religious, cultural, social and personal. Our brothers and sisters behind the bamboo and iron curtains inspire us with their faithfulness to God. May their examples move us to pray all the more that the Holy Spirit would prepare us to follow him across these walls for his sake.

Stone walls do not a prison make,
Nor iron bars a cage.

These lines from "To Althea from Prison" were written by Richard Lovelace, a Royalist prisoner during the seventeenth-century Civil War in England. They echo the apostle Paul's conviction in 2 Timothy 2:9—"I am suffering for [the gospel] even to the point of being chained like a criminal. But God's word is not fettered."

9

PEOPLE PROBLEMS

WHAT? DO MISSIONARIES have people problems too? Yes, because people are as human on one side of the ocean as on the other. Any major change of life, which is what new missionaries must expect, brings new challenges. Some are expected, like adjustments to a new culture and to new coworkers. Others are subtle, like how to get through mundane chores and other "minor" problems common to everybody. These can become serious difficulties and trials which can frustrate or even terminate a missionary's service.

Tensions within the Family
A missionary housemate (with whom I shared many a tear and frustration in trying to work through problems with colleagues),

passed this on to me:
> O to dwell with the saints in heav'n,
> That will be true glory!
> But to dwell with them here on earth,
> That's another story.

I would rather not even say that missionaries have problems with each other. But they do. Indeed, as we have seen in chapter three, three out of four say it is their greatest problem. Some would deny it at first—or give it a euphemistic name—because they do not want to believe it is true, certainly not of themselves. And, of course, no one mentions these matters in prayer letters. It would be indiscreet, and support would plummet.

Somehow, though, God's work goes on despite our human frailties. This is not saying that missionaries are always at each other's throats. It is more likely that the resentment, jealousy or envy is seething below like a volcano. We all know how this saps our emotional energies and diverts us from doing our best work. A missionary to Africa told me that her greatest adjustment was not the language, nor the food, nor the climate, nor the local people. Her major adjustment was to her roommate from her own country. They had to share one big room. Soon each became jealous of space—territorial imperatives, no less. Tensions became electric though nothing was said. How did they solve the problem? By praying? No. Instead, one of them drew a chalk line down the middle of the room so their possessions and they themselves would not get in each other's way, at least not physically. After that they communicated only with curt, necessary phrases.

Is it easier for married couples? Maybe. They have different ways of solving their tensions. For a brief while I lived with a lovely couple. Their children were off at boarding school (another possible source of tension). I thoroughly enjoyed their companionship, except for the heated arguments at breakfast. Not at lunch, not at supper, only at breakfast. They told me that when things get too tense around the house, he goes on an out-of-town evangelistic trip for several days. He forgets the (minor) problem, his wife misses him terribly and people get converted. Then they can make up.

Forgiveness. Why does it disappear when we most need it? It's our pride, the pride of our sweet, stinking self. But the Lord Jesus is not surprised about the things that go on among missionaries—or any group of Christians. He lived in the same atmosphere of family tension with the Twelve. He tells us exactly the same thing that he told them. Without forgiveness there is no hope for change. "For if you forgive men when they sin against you, your heavenly Father will also forgive you. But if you do not forgive men their sins, your Father will not forgive your sins" (Mt 6:14-15). If we haven't learned to forgive again and again and again while we are home, it will be twice as hard overseas.

It's not only those who have directly offended us that we need to forgive. Will we be able to forgive Brenda? She is experienced, and appreciated for her work and abilities. She is not insecure, has no inferiority complex. But Brenda gives others an inferiority complex. If only she were proud, we would have something against her. But her effervescent personality makes everyone else seem dull. We should thank God for these scintillating lights! We could use a few more.

Tensions within Oneself

Tensions in the field are not essentially different from those at home. The major source of family tensions are the tensions *within* individual members. And unfamiliar circumstances bring out greater insecurity and compound personal problems. This can lead to loneliness and, ultimately, to depression. Interpersonal conflicts are often a symptom of loneliness. Because there are fewer familiar escapes, fewer personal distractions that could help them get over some hurdles (even temporarily), loneliness can hit overseas workers in a devastating way. They may be surrounded by many people, supposedly with similar goals. But the fulfillment of others only makes them feel even more emotionally isolated. They begin to resent others' joy, their facility in the language and their friendly relations to the local people.

How does it start? Here's a common route. Bryan feels inadequate in the new language. He tries, makes mistakes and people laugh. He gets frustrated and loses interest in language study. This only aggravates his problem because he cannot communicate effectively with the local people he came to serve. Then he feels guilty. Bryan thinks about his supporters at home. That only makes him feel more guilty. He becomes morose and does not want to be with people at all.

But this path to defeat is avoidable. More experienced colleagues can usually detect the symptoms. Often, however, they are too busy to help. They pray and hope for a change, but they are not able to spend enough quality time with him as a friend.

Often, all it takes is just one friend to turn a lonely, depressed missionary around. In Helen's case, the problems of adjustment were tripled because she was a Hong Kong Chinese in a British-American mission, working in Indonesia. As she groaned in despair, "I have three cultural barriers to cross." Several times she contemplated resigning. But when I saw her about a year later, she was a changed person. A new housemate from the West had become a good friend. With a radiant smile, she exclaimed, "She's always teaching me new Western dishes to cook!"

Loneliness is a terribly private, often hidden, condition. Knowing that it is the most basic problem of human existence (Gen 3) has helped me. None of us is immune to its infection. But certain temperaments are more deeply affected than others. Candidates for overseas work should find out with the help of others whether they can stand being alone for a long time. Can they entertain themselves, keeping creatively occupied when there is no one else around?

This is why you should now develop cultural interests and hobbies that are exportable. Inspired by John Stott, many missionaries have invested in a pair of binoculars for birdwatching. It's cheap, educational, progressive and back-to-nature recreation. For most of my years overseas, I lived out of a suitcase, so music and gardening were temporarily out for me. (I was not yet into carpentry.) I needed a portable weightless hobby. I began experimenting with *haiku,* a three-line, seventeen-syllable form of Japanese poetry. It takes no space in a suitcase. It is mainly in one's head and in nature, and there is always a scrap of paper nearby. It employs one's powers of observation and reflection. It satisfies my needs for relaxation, beauty and creative expression.

Flexibility and a sense of humor are also effective against depression. Missionary life is a series of unexpected happenings. Can we learn from new and changing situations? Can we adapt to new people well enough to make new friends? Or do we tend to make friends with only one type of people? Those who consider themselves intellectuals, for instance, should beware. A sense of humor reveals a sense of balance and proportion. Are we able to laugh at ourselves? Can we keep failure in perspective because we know there is much more to life? Humor is a gift from God that all missionaries must take to the field.

It is no secret that thirty-five to fifty per cent of first-term missionaries return early or do not return after their first term.[10] That in itself is a serious and costly problem to any organization. But think of those returning missionaries themselves, how their personality problems are compounded at home with a sense of failure and often of shame. We must work hard to minimize this problem and to deal with it effectively in the field.

Getting Along with the Boss

"What common problems have you observed among missionaries in west Africa?" I asked a friend. Marilyn works as a Bible translator in Senegal with her denominational mission. I had always respected her keen perceptions and admired the way she could speak with a rare combination of objectivity and compassion. She thoughtfully replied, "The problem of submission to authority." Marilyn went on to make the observation that people she knew with this problem almost invariably had had problems relating to their fathers. This is not a startling, new insight. But it is troubling to know how often this unsolved problem is among the baggage missionaries bring with them. That baggage gets unpacked sooner or later. The problem is indeed common. But I know from personal experience that it can be solved for God's glory and our liberation.

Later I will say something about working under national leaders. Here I want to talk about relationships to one's organizational supervisor. I have had, thank God, very good, imperfect bosses. Over the years, they happened to be (in unique succession) Australian, American, English, Singaporean and Filipino. Each was high-powered and overloaded with responsibilities. Each had a gift of prophecy, for they were always seeing more work that could be done by me for God's kingdom. None were perfect administrators because they enjoyed using their other gifts. Our ideas did not always mesh. With one there occasionally were fierce arguments. But we never got angry at the same time and, thank God, we usually could laugh afterward.

Maybe because we were culturally different, we worked harder on our relationships. Maybe it helped that we did not see each other all the time, as our ministries kept us flying in different orbits. But we kept in touch through correspondence and reports. That is important.

If they frustrated me (that was my most frequent problem), it restrained me to think, Oh, dear, I bet I frustrate them too. Or, I bet it is harder on their wives. If I saw something in them I did not like, I would think, What obnoxious things do they see in me? They were each different from me in temperament and workstyle. What was most important, however, was that we totally agreed in seeking God's kingdom and his righteousness. So we were willing to be subject to one another.

I have said all this because it breaks my heart to see any part of God's work damaged or restrained because of insubordination. For the sake of the work, it is absolutely necessary for us to be loyal to our bosses. At the same time, we are siblings in God's family, not just boss and subordinate. Disloyalty to one's supervisor is one of Satan's most effective weapons for destroying a work. To criticize or talk about him in any way that makes others think less highly of him is sin that demands repentance and forgiveness. I put it that strongly precisely because I have seen the damaging effects. Other people's minds were unwillingly poisoned, and eventually that part of God's work came to a grinding halt. If something is wrong, we know what the Bible teaches about how to right it. And it is never through backbiting and rebellious attitudes.

What has your attitude to your boss or any other authority been like? Positive, negative or just so-so? Missionaries are called to follow Jesus Christ anywhere. That means he asks us to follow him not only to new countries but also into new and difficult relationships.

Praying with Colleagues and Supporters
Some of the dullest prayer meetings I've participated in have been with missionaries. Nothing happened week after week. Some of the most Spirit-moved ones were also with missionaries. *Everything* seemed to be happening!

Praying with colleagues regularly is essential for unity in the work as well as in the fellowship. When missionaries consider prayer optional, they have begun to tread a slippery path. Prayer meetings do not automatically dissolve the interpersonal conflicts we have discussed in this chapter. But people who keep their lives open to God and to others in prayer are better prepared to handle those tensions.

Test yourself in this area. Do you belong to a regular prayer group? You should. What if the prayer meetings are indeed dull? Well, how do changes come in any kind of desperate situation? When one person is agitated enough and cares enough to take the initiative to do something about it. One person can begin by praying that the Spirit of God will awaken all hearts, beginning with his or her own. God delights to answer such prayers.

There is a particular daily prayer meeting I always make every effort to attend when I visit a certain town. Perhaps because it is only for twenty minutes, we try not to waste one minute in chitchat. We always get right down to business with the Lord. It seems like answers to prayer come tumbling down all over the place all the time—for big things. Like sending the right workers, conversions of parents and friends, bringing in enough money for next month's salaries.

For me, one of the greatest encouragements for intercession and mutual prayer support comes from a young colleague in that prayer meeting. Pete would never say that he has the gift of evangelism, but he certainly has the heart for it. He is always enthusiastically asking prayer for this or that friend, project or trip. No one feels Pete is hogging the prayer platform. "He who squeaks gets oiled." Pete asks the most and he receives the most. I would like to be greedy for prayer as Pete is.

Letter Writing and Other Disciplines
Missionary candidates need to learn the discipline of letter writing. Keeping in touch with supporters is vital. Letter writing can be a creative challenge. A missionary must consider, How can I make my situation real to others thousands of miles away? How can I write with a personal touch and yet not bring undue attention to myself? How do I avoid sensationalism and still describe a local event vividly? How do I write about unbelievers without sounding patronizing?

Prayer letters are the bane and blessing of missionaries. They are a bane when one keeps putting off writing them. They are a bane when one struggles to impress others with a catalog of achievements. But they are a blessing when one can truly share God's goodness in mission achievements, his faithfulness in personal insights and problems, and his presence for mutual encouragement and upbuilding.

Among the missionary letters (that you should be receiving regularly) which ones grab you? Why? Prayer letters should be realistic, but should not go on and on describing cultural shock and hinting at personal sacrifices. They should not make "people in the village" sound like inhabitants of another planet. Rather they should convey the feeling that we are all—missionaries, nationals and supporters—on the same planet with the same human problems and the same human aspirations. Prayer letters should indicate to supporters that missionaries are praying for them also. They owe at least this much to their supporters. That is what helps to promote a true missionary *fellowship*.

Caring for people—colleagues, nationals, supporters, family—takes time. How do missionaries make time for people *in* and *beyond* their work and daily chores? In my travels, I have observed all kinds of household hints and time-saving habits from friends I have lived with temporarily. One, an extremely busy scientist, runs her household and garden, keeps vital touch with her local church and manages some real estate. In the mornings, between her quiet time and departure for her laboratory, she follows a simple rule—do four five-minute jobs in twenty minutes. Of course, this has variations. She cleans out one drawer, not four. She pulls one patch of weeds, not six. She repairs one item, not two.

Suppose there are thirty letters to answer. Some missionaries like to sit down and answer them all at one time because they have set aside a whole day to do it. In many ways this is practical; it is easier to write about the same basic things to everybody, and then add a more personal note in response to their personal items. For others, it is easier to put aside an hour or so each day or every other day to answer three or four short letters, or one or two longer ones. That way the mountain of letters is manageable.

One more practical point about letter writing. It is not necessary to write about every interesting thing that has happened. I have stopped flattering myself that my friends or even my family pore over long letters from me with avid interest. One vital item well communicated is more memorable and more appreciated than several paragraphs reciting tedious details or making allusions to unfamiliar people.

It is often the small personal jobs left undone that mount up to formidable mountains, not the big missionary task. These mountains arise when we do not know how to arrange our priorities and our time. Learn now at home to distinguish what is important from what is not. You may have to change some habits and rearrange your lifestyle. When I learned to be less neurotic about sanitation and cleanliness, I found I had more time to do the really important things—and still keep my friends. Simple hospitality has saved me from unnecessary wear and tear, so I can be more relaxed with the people themselves.

Ultimately, Jesus' way with the disciples is our model for relationships with colleagues and for the wise use of our time and energy. Being with people, as Jesus was with the Twelve and others, is the reason we take on the tasks and chores of missionary life in the first place.

10

WOMEN
IN MISSIONS

Some of the problems women missionaries have are peculiar to our modern times, so we devote special attention to them in this chapter.

Missionary Male Chauvinism
Among the many things I was naive about as a new missionary was the peculiar status of single *women* missionaries. I first learned about it one day long before the current era of women's liberation. A friend—a single, female second-term missionary—burst forth into sanctified grumbling. Millie's complaint was about her male colleagues' unfairness to single women.

"How so?" I was curious, for the few that I had met from her mission society seemed like decent, law-abiding citizens. She was teaching in their mission's Bible school. She had regular counseling hours. Besides these major responsibilities she was a member of the curriculum committee and the library committee. She gladly assumed these as her missionary work. But at the weekly staff meetings Millie was also expected to take her turn at providing homemade cakes.

This, she felt, was too much. She reasoned that as a single woman she had the same workload as the men. But the men had wives to bake their cakes as well as keep their house, launder their clothes, shop and cook, and do the countless other tasks every housekeeper has. Moreover, their wives also took care of the prayer letters and other correspondence. As her list grew longer, it was clear she had given much thought and emotional energy to this.

As a novice missionary I became confused. The man's role seemed ideal—absolutely free for field work. The wife's homemaking role seemed equally attractive—absolutely free from field work. But then what were the advantages in being a single missionary, without spouse or children, for the ultimate concentration on The Mission?

I do not know whether Millie ever made her point to her male colleagues or just kept dipping sacrificially into her dwindling supply of cake mixes. Had the climate been more like today's, she might have solved her problem by marrying a missionary who could bake her cakes and keep her house.

By no means are all male missionaries like Millie's colleagues. Later, I met male members of other mission societies, and found that missionary men are usually a bit more broad-minded about women in leadership than are many of their counterparts at home. A few rare ones even urged me to get ordained!

Reversed Disproportion and God's Sovereignty

If a single Christian woman is looking for a Christian husband, the mission field is the worst place to go. Currently the proportion among missionaries is something like five women to three men in the better pastures and three women to one and one-half men in the browned-over fields, according to a friend who is still single and available. This is a reversal of the sex ratio in the history of missions. In the great procession of missionaries from the first to the nineteenth centuries, marches one man after the other. Occasionally a skirt appears, but often faceless or as the wife of "the" missionary. Only late in the nineteenth century in America did a tiny but significant stream of women begin to appear. R. Pierce Beaver explains that

the customs of the Oriental peoples made it almost impossible for male missionaries to reach women and with them children in large numbers. Missionary wives endeavored to set up schools for girls and to penetrate the homes, zenanas, and harems, but they did not have enough freedom from home-making and child care and they could not itinerate. Realistic strategy demanded that adequate provision be made for women and children, but the boards and societies were stubbornly resistant to sending single women abroad for such work. Finally in desperation the women in the 1860's began organizing their own societies and sent forth single women. A whole new dimension was added to mission strategy: the vast enterprise to reach women and children with the gospel, to educate girls, and to bring adequate medical care to women.

When women came into the church, their children followed them. Female education proved to be the most effective force for the liberation and social uplift of women. The emphasis which the women placed on medical service led the general boards to upgrade the medical work, and greater stress was put on medical education. Out of these two great endeavors of American women, followed by the British and Europeans, there opened to women of the Orient, what are today their most prestigious professions, medical service both as physicians and nurses, and teaching.[11]

One can draw a valid thesis from this trend: With the increasing liberation of women in the West since the midnineteenth century, the proportion of women in mission forces likewise has increased. Then something subtle began to appear. More and more, women overseas began to find freedom to exercise their gifts in Christ's body that they could not express at home. In God's sovereignty this has helped to bring about greater expansion of his worldwide church. (But the corollary of the decreasing proportion of men serving on the pioneer frontlines has become almost embarrassing.)

From this reversed disproportion of the sexes, two major tensions have developed: (1) the growing strength of female leadership on the field and its effects on their home churches, and (2) the increase of single women missionaries. What are some implications for the church?

Women with Leadership Responsibilities

Christians vary greatly in their views and emotions about women leaders in the church. Their positions usually reflect the social/ cultural groups they come from, whether purely traditional, biblically conservative, cautiously progressive or radically liberal. Likewise, women missionaries generally reflect the views of their denominations and the "faith" missions they choose. The educational institutions they have attended—Bible schools, Christian colleges, private or state universities—also reinforce their cultural tendencies and subsequently their biblical interpretations of women in leadership.

Regardless of their background, however, women on the field usually become more independent than before. Otherwise they would not survive. Neither would their ministries. Some are able to argue persuasively on firm biblical ground why and to what degree they, as Christian women, are exercising the legitimate rediscovered authority through the gifts they have from Christ's Spirit. Others exercise their gifts of leadership with less biblical eloquence but much pragmatism and concern for God's work. There are, of course, also many women who are most comfortable in a traditional role of one-way submission to men and have no desire to use possible gifts of leadership. God bless us all!

Through the years of an intercontinental mission, I have never met with opposition from male leaders, though I clearly exercised some kind of authority. Only once was there indirect opposition. I was teaching for several weeks in a seminary in a strongly patriarchal country. None of the staff objected. But some of the male students had been influenced by a local minister who applied 1 Timothy 2:12 (not allowing a woman to teach or to have authority over man) in a universal and absolute way. They attended my class, however, because I was not teaching Bible doctrine systematically but "only training us in evangelistic Bible studies." Presumably, I exercised no authority over them nor taught them doctrine, however indirectly.

During that week, while I merrily continued my classes, the National Executive Committee met to settle the issue about women teachers. The paper presented by the principal of the seminary pointed out that women had authority to teach as delegated by that very National Committee, which was composed of men who themselves were under the doctrinal statement of faith. At the time that was good enough for me, as I was keen to get on with the work.

Since then I have been more and more frequently asked by younger leaders in the Third World how I reconcile my ministry with the New Testament passages that seem to forbid women leadership in the church. This has been a tremendous challenge. I believe that Christian leaders today cannot avoid rethinking their views on women and women leadership. Is our view essentially influenced by nineteenth-century traditions or by the teaching and practice of the first-century church?

A fair treatment of different positions would require at least another chapter, but it is not necessary here and now. May I sketch briefly how my views have changed through the years? I began with the traditional position that women were never to preach in church, teach men or hold senior leadership positions. But as I observed women at work for God on all continents and began to rethink biblical passages *and patterns* on the subject, I became more and more uneasy. I began to feel a corporate hypocrisy in calling my messages "just sharing" when I spoke behind the pulpit on a Sunday morning. Moreover, I realized that as a counselor or a teacher/trainer in Bible studies and evangelism, I was exerting influence over many young men. Should I terminate my ministry?

As I researched and reviewed the relevant passages from Genesis 1:26-28 to 1 Timothy 2:8-15, I was pushed to question seriously my former understanding. I came to see the issue in its greater biblical context: God's redemptive purpose from Genesis 3 to Revelation 22 is to get us back to Genesis 1:26-28, where male and female have equal responsibilities in exercising dominion over the earth and in making it fruitful. This creation mandate is reinforced and clarified in many New Testament passages (such as 2 Cor 5:17; Gal 3:28; 1 Pet 3:7).

From the beginning of the Christian church, women worked alongside men. Luke 8:1-3 may seem like a tiny episode in the Gospels. But we must see that Jesus, in his male-dominated culture, was being radical in even allowing these women to follow in his itinerant company. Moreover, Luke's record of Jesus' women supporters is only part of the larger, progressive pattern in Jesus' ministry to women, climaxing after his resurrection in his appearing first to women.[12]

Like Jesus his master, Paul was radical in theology but cautiously progressive in its application. The book of Acts and Paul's letters to young churches show apostolic practice of Jesus' example. In one chapter alone, Romans 16, Paul lists nine, possibly ten women out of twenty-nine coworkers whom he appreciated individually for their unique contribution to the planting and nurturing of churches.

I am intrigued by the progress of biblical reinterpretations going on in a historically conservative body of believers, the Christian Brethren (sometimes called Plymouth Brethren). The silence of their women in public worship is about the only characteristic many other Christians know about them. But theirs is a fascinating history outstripping this peculiarity. When they began in the early nineteenth century in Britain, they were the radical evangelicals in the Anglican (Episcopalian) church. They stood for getting back to the centrality of Scripture. They emphasized the importance of the "laity" to the point of discarding any clerical class. (Similar movements were springing up on the continent at the same time.)

Christian Brethren have had an important biblical influence all over the world out of proportion to their numbers. They have always been so mission-minded that one per cent of their members became missionaries. Their overseas work has lasted significantly on all continents in such diverse countries as Argentina, Singapore, South India, Zaire and the United States.[13] Their influence, however, began to wane when some of their practices started to jar with the changing times and, in the view of some of their own leaders, to be inconsistent with Scripture after all.

They have been honest enough to face the issue of women leaders in the church squarely and scripturally. They have been living for decades with an uncomfortable contradiction. Their missionary women were "allowed" to do the traditional work of men in the churches overseas simply because there were no males to preach, teach, pioneer and evangelize. Yet when these same women returned to their home assemblies, they were not allowed to exercise any of their gifts, not even to pray in public, which was clearly an apostolic church practice (1 Cor 11:5).

Once more they are doing some courageous thinking in reconsidering their traditional interpretation of the Bible's position of women in the church. Some of their best thinkers and Bible scholars like F. F. Bruce have an international reputation for sound biblical theology. Many of these are discussing and writing about the right and the need for women to exercise their gifts of leadership and other ministries in the churches.[14]

Once in a while I am urged by friends of both sexes to be ordained as a minister "in order to make a statement" (more self-conscious terminology!). God forbid that I should be complacent or smug, but I have no desire to. I have more leadership and teaching responsibilities than I can now handle. Personally I see no real argument in Scripture against the ordination of women. But neither do I see what it would do for my ministry at the present time. In general I take the position of Paul, who was theologically revolutionary but sociologically cautious. I thank God for my many brothers around the world who constantly affirm my gifts, whether they are my constant colleagues or temporary coworkers. Together we work as partners for God's kingdom. I do not think they feel threatened by me and my ministries because we are fellow servants serving a great king. Him we want to glorify, not either sex.

The Single Blessing

The other result of having a disproportionate number of women missionaries is that of singleness. Nonetheless, singleness does affect both sexes.

Every Christian single person is familiar with the scattered verses in 1 Corinthians 7 about the advantages of being single for the sake of devotion to God and the ministry (verses 8, 25-27, 32-35). Those who do not like these verses hurry on to those others that give a way out (verses 7, 9, 28). Less frequently cited are the words of Jesus himself: "Not everyone can accept this teaching, but only those to whom it has been given. For some are eunuchs because they were born that way; others were made that way by men; and others have renounced marriage because of the kingdom of heaven. The one who can accept this should accept it" (Mt 19:11-12). Like Paul, Jesus also recognizes that not everyone can accept this condition of singleness for the sake of the kingdom of God. But it is given to some.

Many successful missionary projects have been achieved by single men and women. We have just mentioned Jesus and Paul. But the many missionary orders of the monastic tradition are full of examples. Columba of Ireland (521-597), the abbot and missionary born of noble parents, is outstanding. He established a base for evangelism on the Island of Iona to reach his fellow Scots and the Picts. Largely through his efforts, the Celtic church became God's instrument in bringing Christianity to Western Europe after the fall of the Roman Empire. Like Columba, Ignatius of Loyola (1495-1556) was of noble birth. He founded the powerful Society of Jesus (the Jesuits), which to this day exerts a tremendous influence for the Roman Catholic Church in nearly every country of the world.

In modern times we can consider the missionary spinsters who touched a multitude of lives for God, and who, though gone, still influence others by the work they left behind—Amy Carmichael of India, Mary Slessor of Africa, Irene Webster-Smith of Japan. And think of Mother Teresa of Calcutta in our day.

Kingdom Advantages

Yes, the advantages of being single are so unique, so extraordinary, so fantastic that I cannot imagine why missionaries should even think of getting married. That is, until I think of the marvelous advantages of marriage. Seriously, I think the advantages of singleness are so obvious that they are in danger of being overlooked rather than used. What are they?

Concentration. Single missionaries have more potential for concentrating on their ministry than do married people. They have no family life and problems to distract them. Language studies, which demand intense and steady discipline, can be sustained without having to stop to change the baby's diapers or to lose several nights' sleep because of the children's illnesses. Spontaneous evangelistic opportunities can be seized without considering a family schedule. Intense training programs can be focused on without having to divert energy to the personal problems of a marriage partner. The education of the children, the dilemma of bringing them up to feel secure with one culture or another, the psychological problems of teen-age children—I have seen these things drive some gifted and fruitful missionary couples back to their home countries.

But even without children, married missionaries can have devastating problems. A well-loved and fruitful missionary I worked with became frustrated and ineffective after he married while at home on furlough. His wife could not or would not adjust to their new country. She constantly found excuses not to meet his friends; she virtually locked herself in the bedroom. She felt she could not learn the national language, so she did not try. She found it impossible to eat the national food without vomiting later. They returned to their homeland within a year.

This is not to say, of course, that marriage is bad for a missionary. Many of us single missionaries would love to be married to the kind of man or woman with whom we could effectively serve God. We would like to have our cake and eat it too. If there were reincarnation, I would ask to try the married state the next time around.

Nor am I saying that singleness does not have its problems. It certainly does. But a single missionary whose passion is the glory of God has unusual advantages. That is what both Jesus and Paul knew when they spoke about singleness.

Flexibility. Any missionary home is run by clocks and calendars to some degree, especially if they come from the United States. But the schedules of single missionaries are more flexible because they usually consult only themselves about changes. It is much easier, even when they have housemates, to have friends drop in or to skip meals to stay out longer with people who need counsel or friendship. They can make out-of-town evangelistic trips more readily when the opportunities arise.

Community orientation. This more independent scheduling usually means the single missionary can move along more easily with the community life, participating naturally and even regularly in cultural activities. I once went to a student leadership camp in Malaysia. On fun night the highlight of the program was an Indonesian folk dance by a missionary. She danced with grace and skill that won spontaneous applause. I thought she must have been a professional dancer before becoming a missionary. She tossed off our compliments with, "Oh, I just learned this in my spare time with my Indonesian friends." I have no doubt that this is one of the reasons she and her teaching ministry are so well accepted in her appointed country.

The uncluttered life. It is easier for the single missionary to maintain a simple life. I always feel tired, though quite sympathetic, just watching a missionary family packing or unpacking suitcases and trunks. They need family things that a single person does not, more furnishings to make "a home," more clothes, more medicine and particularly more things for the children.

Singles can get along with temporary furnishings that are impractical for a family. They can live out of a suitcase but a family cannot. A bicycle often suffices for a single person, but a family usually has to have a car. So not only do singles spend less money on personal and household furnishings; they spend less time maintaining them. In short, singles can keep their lives uncluttered materially and mentally. This should make it easier to keep their lives emotionally uncluttered too.

Mobility. Although most missionaries have their own homes, some have a mobile ministry. When single missionaries go on out-of-town trips and stay away for days or weeks, there is no disruption of family life. Singles also can better adapt to sudden changes.

But, of course, these fabulous single missionaries I have been picturing are not as plentiful as we wish. For alas, singles face their unique problems, just as married persons do.

Disadvantages and Challenges

When I speak of the problems and temptations of single persons, married friends sometimes say, "They are basically the same as ours." Though I have always known that marriage does not automatically solve all one's problems and meet all one's needs, it is better for a married person to say that than a single person. But we still need to reflect on these issues *in the single context,* though I cannot treat them in detail.

Self-orientation. The demands on a missionary's life and ministry bring out the best and the worst in us, as I have tried to show in earlier chapters. We become more and more of what we have always tended to be. If we have had a tendency to be self-centered and petty, we will become, apart from the grace of God, more so in the tensions of a new life.

Single people have basically only themselves to think about in the planning of meals, budget, holidays and decorating the house. They can become more private people, closing themselves to others except for their "professional" work. Many missionary women like to live alone if possible. This is understandable, for every woman wants to have her own home. The danger is in becoming too independent and less interdependent in the body of Christ.

Sex and marriage tensions. What do I do with my natural sex drives and desire for the permanent, intimate companionship of a husband or wife? When these are out of control, our best energies are channeled away from constructive work and activities. The problem can come out in heterosexual or homosexual attractions in the remoteness of a lonely situation. The dangers are there, and mission supervisors are generally not blind to the possibilities. That does not mean that every single missionary is in constant sexual tension. As a matter of fact, missionary work is a healthy sublimation because it means giving oneself to others in a positive way.

Naturally these desires raise the possibility of romance and marriage with a national believer. We are likely to see more and more of such intercultural unions. And I would not be surprised if this is one of God's ways of hastening international partnership in mission. Many of these marriages are truly blessed. The couple are doubly effective in witness and work. But this demands great maturity on both sides.

Some intercultural marriages have been disasters or have produced quiet desperation after the romance evaporated in the realities of deeper crosscultural problems. Often the families are not reconciled to the idea. Neither partner feels comfortable in the other's family and community. And where are they to live? An intercultural marriage has greater than usual adjustments to work through. Some simply do not make it. Here, all the more, marriage is not to be entered into lightly.

When I have been tempted to feel sorry for myself in this area of singleness, the greatest help has been to ask, "How did those bachelor missionaries, Jesus and Paul, handle this problem?" They vigorously used their passions for God, actively loving and helping people into the kingdom.

Mediocrity. Married missionaries can check each other's faults and encourage each other's strengths. But singles often have no one to objectively and regularly evaluate their progress. Thus, singles may slide subtly into mediocrity. From heat and humidity, and battle fatigue, more and more they take the path of least resistance. They lower their standards. They pray less, work less. They spend fewer hours in preparation, no longer take time to think creatively. They become satisfied with mediocrity, just spinning the wheel, motion without direction.

Care for family. Some time ago I arrived in a city, hoping to work with a missionary sister. We had been corresponding for a year, planning for a joint ministry. She had been quite successful in starting Bible study groups and turning them over to trained leaders. And there was more work to be done. I was disappointed when she suddenly had to return to her home country. Her sick, widowed mother had taken a turn for the worse and was becoming senile and helpless. Other sisters and brothers were married and had children. She was the only unmarried one, who should "of course" take care of Mother. I sat down in dismay not because I now had no one to work with, but because she was the third missionary friend within that year to go home for the same reason.

Retirement. As singles move toward middle age, they have to consider seriously how much longer they can be effective in their present ministry. The national churches and their home countries are rapidly changing. Some begin to feel that they do not fit in either place. As the national church matures, are they able to change their ministry? Are they getting in the way of local progress? Should they move to another field? Get more training? Return home to work? If so, church or secular work? These are hard realities to face alone. Singles often do not have a companion with whom to face the future and make plans for eventual retirement. Many single missionaries do not have the finances to be independent in old age. Nor do they want to be a burden to relatives, especially if they are not believers. All they can look forward to is a missionary retirement home. Some may like that. Others may dread it but have no choice.

Fulfillment. At every stage of life, in every state—whether married or single, male or female—with God there is always the possibility of a fulfilled life. That is God's loving aim for all his children. Although I meet many missionaries who are frustrated by lack of apparent success, by unsatisfied natural longings for a mate, by male chauvinism, I also know many, many more who are deeply contented people, full-orbed in their warm humanity. They are experiencing a sense of achievement because they have sought to please God. Like the apostle Paul they are living out their chosen priorities that bring the greatest, lasting reward— oneness with Jesus their Lord. "But whatever was to my profit I now consider loss for the sake of Christ. What is more, I consider everything a loss compared to the surpassing greatness of knowing Christ Jesus my Lord, for whose sake I have lost all things. I consider them rubbish, that I may gain Christ and be found in him" (Phil 3:7-9).

11

MISSIONS IN TRANSITION

IN THE COURSE OF WORKING with students in a new country, I am frequently asked, "Where is your headquarters?" When I answer, "We have none, but we do have an administrative service office in London," I get puzzled looks. Then I am glad for the opportunity to explain the philosophy of our work.

These young people find it difficult to believe that we really mean it when we say that we are there mainly to help them develop their own national movement without outside controls. Like their Christian elders, they assume that all missionaries get their directives from some headquarters in the West (or North, if they're in Africa or Latin America).

But sometimes we come across someone who does not believe us at all. He has made up his mind, like Nathanael in John 1:46—

"The West! Can any good come out of it?" My boss Chua Wee Hian and I met such a Nathanael. We were on a rare trip together to a new movement which had asked for our help. When we arrived in the capital, we found among the young people a widespread awakening of Pentecost-like proportions. We felt like Barnabas in Acts 11:23: "When he arrived and saw the evidence of the grace of God, he was glad and encouraged them all to remain true to the Lord with all their hearts."

Wee Hian gave Bible expositions, and I ran workshops on evangelistic Bible studies. We were busy all day and sometimes half the night counseling eager students and graduates. It seemed they could not get enough. They loved hearing about Christian students like themselves witnessing for Jesus Christ in universities around the world. When they asked if they could join this fellowship officially, Wee Hian explained the conditions. They were delighted.

Enter the gadfly, the chairman of the group no less. Bright, articulate, handsome, respected. "You came here just to build your empire. You are only interested in adding our organization to your Western empire. Then you can write to your financial supporters and tell them about your successes. Then they will give you more money. Every missionary organization has imperialistic motives."

Had I been alone, I would have shriveled up like batter in hot oil. I let the boss do all the talking. Wee Hian gently pointed out that every member movement in the fellowship is independent. He added that together the members like themselves elected an international executive committee as the authority above all us staff. That was all that could be done at that emotional point. Soon afterward, however, Wee Hian encouraged another movement on the same continent to invite representatives from this new movement to participate in their annual leadership training camp. The handsome chairman was among those who went.

About a year later, Wee Hian received a letter from him apologizing for his previous stand and applying for membership on behalf of their movement. He explained that his first reaction was like that of many others in his generation. His father had been a minister "under a white mission." He had seen his father virtually become their servant and silently bear indignities to his person. While he realized he was himself indebted to the coming of the white missionaries for his salvation, he had determined never to be further indebted to them or to be associated with them.

Aspects of Transition
The incident of the handsome chairman is symbolic of some aspects of the transition that missionary work is going through, at least in the Third World.[15] While student evangelism and their leadership training do not represent all missionary work, they are nevertheless strategic areas within younger churches in that world and ours.

Mission organizations have generally established national churches in most countries to which they have gone. Notable exceptions are the Islamic countries. The local pastors and evangelists, however, have usually not had the tertiary education that could prepare them for the changes of the fast-paced modern world. On the other hand, their young people today are having opportunities for tertiary education, so for the first time in most of these churches there are university-educated members. Professional people are more commonly seen in the pews.

In spite of the education gap between them and their pastors, most university graduates have stayed with their churches. This is probably because of strong family loyalties and community ties. But in many countries it has been hard to attract new people to the same churches. God in his sovereign grace has been raising up evangelical student movements that are not only helping young Christians remain in the churches. They are also reaching non-Christians for the churches. They are providing new leadership and new impetus for the churches, Bible schools and seminaries.

National prejudices against missions are aggravated not only by Western mistakes and attitudes but also by nationalistic feelings expressed by a more articulate generation. We must deal with these prejudices wisely. Both sides should confess where they have been wrong. We should preserve the good of the past and build on it by working together determinedly. Fortunately, westerners are not the only missionaries. On all continents, God has been silently sending men and women into all the world to make disciples of all nations. Later in this chapter I will discuss this in more detail.

Rising Expectations
Trends and tensions in the political world also are often reflected in national church/mission organization relationships. After World War 2, for example, the great European empires began to be dismantled on all continents. At this time also, the United States left the Philippines after an occupation of almost fifty years there. New nations were born, and older nations were reborn as they gained or regained independence from the colonial powers. Political leadership was at last in the hands of the people.

Parallel to this political change, many mission organizations were pressured to release more and more of their control. "Indigenous churches" and "indigenous leadership" were popular concepts: sometimes they were put into practice prematurely. In some cases, the missionaries had not prepared the nationals for organizational or spiritual independence. Why were many of them caught unprepared? Why did it take international political changes to make mission organizations do what, according to the New Testament pattern, they should have done years before? It is sad that so often the world has to lead the church, instead of the other way around.

But political independence for these young or reborn nations has not always meant economic independence. "Rising expectations" is a phrase often used in connection with emerging nations. With their new political powers, they also want more material goods and more influence in the world community. They have seen their natural resources plundered and squandered to sustain the ever-rising standard of living in prosperous developed countries. They want a share in the fruit of the technology that their raw materials helped to produce. But how? They are poorer now than ever.

"Rising expectations" also applies to young Christians being trained for the ministry. When these young Christians are trained by affluent mission organizations, their expectations can be expressed in unhealthy ways. In a Southeast Asian country, a seminary professor from such a mission organization came to visit my host and his family. It was the end of a demanding seminary year. He should have been relieved. But instead, he was troubled by the results of an evaluation form he had asked the graduating class of six to fill out. One of the questions was, "How would you like the (denominational) mission to help you in your future ministry?" They answered in similar fashion. Each expected (1) a salary about five times that of the average national pastor, (2) a house like the missionary's and (3) a motorbike. At least they did not suggest a Land Rover like the missionary's.

Tentmaking

Another kind of missionary work is tentmaking. Instead of going as full-time or professional missionaries, tentmakers work in their own professions or some other job. As nonprofessional missionaries they support themselves, witness through their work and do other Christian ministry in their off-hours. A generation ago tentmaking would not have gained much of a response from Christians and churches or mission organizations. But today there is increasing discussion and implementation of this "new" kind of missionary work.

Our work in the Philippines got off to an excellent start with a solid nucleus of six to eight students and Gwen, a great pioneer worker. As the work expanded, Mary, another pioneer worker, joined her. Gwen and Mary, however, would be the first to credit a tentmaking couple with helping to lay the solid foundations of that work which lasts to this day. Peter was fully employed by

Shell Oil Company, and his wife Evelyn was equally occupied with family responsibilities. But evenings, weekends, holidays and vacations were devoted especially to strengthening the graduate area of the movement.

The biblical progenitors of this American-British couple are Priscilla and Aquila. Acts 18 tells the story of this Jewish couple from Rome who came to Corinth. It was at that moment that the great apostle Paul was facing one of the most discouraging situations in his missionary career. Verse 3 says that "because he was a tentmaker as they were, he stayed and worked with them." They may have already been Christians by the time they arrived in Corinth, or they may have become believers through Paul in this contact. In either case, they gave him the encouragement he needed. They provided a home for him, and they became vitally involved in evangelism and follow-up work with him.

God has had his stream of tentmakers since then, fanning throughout the world. Sometimes that has been the only way the gospel could enter and his church be established in certain countries or localities. Muslim Afghanistan is such a country. Dr. and Mrs. J. Christy Wilson, Jr., went there for four years as teachers. In his helpful and highly readable book *Today's Tentmakers* he reports that there are over one million American Christians living and working in other countries as engineers, accountants, doctors, agriculturists, or studying in the universities there. Since he reported that in 1979, thousands more have gone abroad in similar capacities with similar purposes. China especially has been attracting hundreds of young Christians to teach English.

The Overseas Counseling Service (1594 N. Allen, #23, Pasadena, CA 91104) devotes its entire ministry to providing information to inquirers about such tentmaking possibilities in various countries. Its brochures and newsletters often refer to the fact that sixty per cent of the countries in the world do not allow traditional missionaries to enter as such. More mission organizations are promoting this alternative for worldwide witness.

Non-Western Missions
Another change in missions during our generation is the indigenous and independent work being done by people who do not write prayer letters! Anyone who knows anything about the house churches in China, for example, is aware of God's new thrust. This is happening in varying degrees on every continent. At a Brazilian missionary conference several years ago, we heard many excellent speakers. To this day the ones I best remember were the Brazilian and Peruvian nonprofessional missionaries. They had gone as small teams of doctors and nurses, engineers and teachers, even journalists and psychologists. Their aim was to live among the people in the remote towns and villages, serving them and sharing the good news with them, so they could build their own churches.

A few years ago, a Bolivian student studying in Brazil became a Christian through the witness of Christians on his campus. He grew spiritually. He caught a vision for his own country where there was not yet a campus Christian witness. Today he is fully occupied in pioneer evangelism back in the universities of Bolivia.

Indigenous missionary conferences are taking place on all continents. National mission societies have been formed in many well-known mission fields. I heard Theodore Williams, a leading Indian missiologist, report that his country has over one hundred. God has been using these to gently push Asians, Africans and Latin American Christians over their borders to other countries in their region or to other continents. Christians all over the world are more and more seeing themselves no longer as receivers of missionaries but as senders.

Greek Christians with a sense of Christ's mission are praying for some kind of opening into the atheistic state of Albania, their neighbors to the northwest. Some of them are already quietly witnessing to their other neighbors in Yugoslavia. The central African country of Zambia shares borders with Angola and Mozambique, both former Portuguese colonies which at present have Marxist-led governments. Zambian Christians have also been quietly slipping in and out to strengthen the weakened churches there. The same is true for some Christians from Zimbabwe and South Africa, which are neighbors to Mozambique.

The prayer sheet, "The Church around the World," from Tyndale House reported in October 1982 that "15,000 Third World missionaries from 57 countries account for one-third of the total world full-time missionary force. Non-Western missionary recruitment for full-time crosscultural endeavor is growing five times as fast as missionary recruitment in North America. One major problem, however, is the high one-term fallout among Third World missionaries due to the lack of financial support." The last statement should provoke more discussion on practical international cooperation in world mission.

Does this mean then that the day of *Western* missionaries is over? Yes, if we mean the exclusivistic mindset of many in the pre-World War 2 era of missions. No, if we mean a genuine participation in a new era of international partnership.

International Teamwork
What makes missions doubly challenging today is that we work in closer partnership with leaders from many nations and cultures. For eighteenth- and nineteenth-century missionaries this would have been almost impossible to imagine, though they labored sacrificially to lay down the foundation for us.

Today we are being forced to think in different ways. We must rearrange our mental categories. We need to ask and answer honestly, What does the history of missions teach us? What indeed are the mistakes we have made? How willing are we to go back humbly to square one? In an All India Missionary Conference in Nagpur, I heard an Indian brother admonish his fellow Christians that they were not getting the gospel out faster because they still had unregenerate Hindu minds. I wonder if it could be said that some of us still have an unregenerate Western mind concerning missions?[16]

The Lausanne Congress on World Evangelization in 1974

highlighted this trend of international cooperation that had been taking place since the end of World War 2. The Lausanne Congress itself—with 2700 participants from most of the countries in the world—made great strides toward partnership in missions. There were tensions, however, for some in the West could not accept that the way they had been doing missionary work should be different. The preaching of the gospel, for instance, must be accompanied equally by caring for the poor and the oppressed. Perhaps some missionaries also felt insecure about their past paternalistic role and fearful that they would be reduced to mere equality with non-Western church leaders. Lausanne was worthwhile, if only because such tensions were brought to international attention. Since then, mission organizations and evangelistic teams have worked harder at resolving these issues.

New missionaries, however, do not usually attend these high-powered conferences. Many still go overseas with all kinds of inherited, pre-World War 2 conceptions. They expect to work with "the natives," even though this term has been replaced by "the nationals." Intellectually, they understand the great changes that have been taking place—they may have attended an Urbana conference or two.[17] But they have not yet had enough cultural confrontations and deep personal struggles with others to experience the necessary emotional changes.

One of these new missionaries, who is now more seasoned and wiser after a few struggles, told me about her early struggle with true hospitality in a capital city in east Africa. During their first year she and her husband let it be known that their home was open to all—in true African hospitality. Then she was asked by a local Christian worker to house some who had come for a regional conference. When she learned that they were young people, she felt she had to lay down the rules: no radio playing; no coming in after 10:00 P.M.; no use of the living room; no use of the family bathroom, but the servant's was available; and above all, no use of the family's cassettes, some of which had been ruined by the last group of guests. Otherwise, they were welcome. She was being practical, she thought. The African worker simply responded, "What did you come to Africa for?" Admittedly, this response is not typical. But I daresay there will be more outspoken ones like it in the near future.

12

WHEN OUR WORK IS DONE

Let's be concerned with training servants, and God will train the leaders." In one sense, this statement by Dr. V. Raymond Edman, former president of Wheaton College, is correct: we do not train leaders, but servants. Christian leaders must be servants. Yet the Bible is clear about learning to "pass it on" (2 Tim 2:2). This is what training disciple makers is about.

Missionary work is as strong as its leadership training. In advanced work this can be structured training as in a Bible school or seminary for pastors and preachers. Or it can be informal, life-upon-life contacts which leave guaranteed-for-life impressions. Jesus' most profound training of the Twelve was nonverbal. His example was powerful, reinforcing his words; his passionate spirit penetrated them. They could never again be the same.

So essential is training disciples and disciple makers in a missionary program that candidates should question their missionary call if they cannot train or help others to train. Is not this just common sense about how God's work is continued? It is sobering to realize that a work is always one generation away from extinction.

A friend shared this paraphrase of Psalm 90:12 from his German Bible: "Teach us to consider that someday we must die, so that we may live wisely." Coretta Scott King said her huband, Martin Luther King, Jr., always knew he would someday die suddenly. The question was when, not if. Jesus too knew that his death had been planned. It did not come suddenly. His limited time with the Twelve was a high priority. But there was no rush, no panic. He refused to let the Twelve or others pressure him to follow their schedule. (For example, Mk 1:35-39; 5:22-43; 6:35-36 and Lk 13:31-32.)

The student work in Thailand was one of the last in Southeast Asia to begin to move. The Christians in the total population of that country have been outnumbered by the number of Buddhist temples. At last, with the vision and careful planning of a Scottish missionary, a lecturer in pharmacy at the University of Chulalongkorn, a small handful of Christians formed an evangelistic nucleus. They caught his vision. This was exciting to all who for years had been watching, praying and doing what they could. The student leader of the tiny nucleus was ideal for such an uphill work. He was energetic, evangelistic and inspiring to the others. Then, suddenly, he was killed in a car accident while returning from an evangelistic meeting in another town. None of the five or six other students seemed the type to lead on. Back to square one.

Or so we first thought. God used his death to make his evangelistic example even clearer. Others rose up one by one, slowly but surely. It took a long time, but the evangelistic movement in the high schools and universities has spread to other cities and towns of Thailand, and they have been raising up their own leaders. "The hour has come for the Son of Man to be glorified. I tell you the truth, unless a kernel of wheat falls to the ground and dies, it remains only a single seed. But if it dies, it produces many seeds" (Jn 12:23-24).

Missionaries Must Die

Missionaries too should keep their death in mind, not morbidly but cheerfully. If not physically, then at least psychologically. For we should always be aiming to so teach and train people that they can carry on God's work on earth without our presence. I know of at least two missionaries who knew when they had finished a particular mission and were glad to move to another assignment.

The first is Jesus. When he prayed his intercessory prayer for the Twelve (Jn 17), he had already completed their training. We see this most clearly in verse 18.

I have revealed you [Father] to those whom you gave me out of the world. They were yours; you gave them to me and they have obeyed your word. Now they know that everything you have given me comes from you. For I gave them the words you gave me and they accepted them. They knew with certainty that I came from you, and they believed that you sent me. . . . I will remain in the world no longer, but they are still in the world, and I am coming to you. . . . As you sent me into the world, I have sent them into the world. (Jn 17:6-8, 11, 18)

If Jesus' example sounds too noble for you, then consider Paul, my second example. At the end of their first overseas mission, Paul and Barnabas knew when they could safely leave the work to local leaders (Acts 14:21-28). And they did. But it is also highly significant how they began their next missionary term after their furlough in Antioch: "Let us go back and visit the brothers in all the towns where we preached the word of the Lord and see how they are doing" (Acts 15:36).

Not only at the end of a geographical assignment, but at the end of his life, Paul turned over his work to younger coworkers like Timothy. This time, however, there would be no return trip to check on Timothy and others. He's leaving for good.

For I am already being poured out like a drink offering, and the time has come for my departure. I have fought the good fight, I have finished the race, I have kept the faith. Now there is in store for me the crown of righteousness, which the Lord, the righteous Judge, will award to me on that day. (2 Tim 4:6-8)

In this light we can understand better his no-nonsense commands.

In the presence of God and of Christ Jesus, who will judge the living and the dead, and in view of his appearing and his kingdom, I give you this charge: Preach the Word; be prepared in season and out of season; correct, rebuke and encourage. . . .

Keep your head in all situations, endure hardship, do the work of an evangelist, discharge all the duties of your ministry. (2 Tim 4:1-2, 5)

The issue of death should be a creative tension for us, challenging us to keep alert in our task of growing disciple makers.

Who's in Charge?

It is time for missionaries to leave when they can turn over the work to others. Not one year sooner, not one year later. Like Paul and Barnabas, they may return, if it is helpful, for a special assignment for a defined period. But it must be clear who is in charge. Otherwise, their presence may restrain the further growth of local leadership and initiative.

Sometimes it is not a matter of leaving the country, but stepping down from an administrative position to work under a national leader. I know of one who was pastor of a young church he had helped to found. After about five years, he gave it up to return to his first love—evangelism. This meant he worked under the new pastor, a former deacon who was much younger than he. The missionary, however, had been such a poor administrator that the young national pastor was not at all threatened!

The Philippine IVCF was once criticized for insisting on being an indigenous movement, while retaining American and British missionaries on their staff (three or four out of thirty). Dr. Isabelo Magalit, the general secretary then, replied, "We *are* an indigenous movement. Leadership and responsibilities are in the hands of Filipinos. But to get God's work done we need a team of people with different gifts. We look first for Filipinos. If no one of us has a certain needed gift, then we welcome any brother or sister from any country who has that gift to contribute." This certainly was true of the Antiochan church, whose leaders were interracial and international.

Not all missionaries find it easy to fit into a team under national leadership. Though no one says it aloud, they would be expected to live by their national coworkers' material standards as far as possible. This would mean a radical drop in the standard of living for many missionaries. But many are doing it; it *is* possible. At the same time, I have observed that it is the missionary's *attitude,* rather than the *quantity* of possessions, that makes the difference. Does she cling inordinately to her Western way of life? Or does he share whatever he has with others? As long as the standard of living is not conspicuously different, most local Christians understand that Western missionaries have certain needs which the nationals do not have.

Some missionaries just cannot work under national leadership. One brother tried hard for three years. He was a gifted worker, able to spend hours with nonbelievers before they turned to Christ. He was not a proud person. He lived as simply as the townspeople whom he loved and who loved him. But he finally had to ask his mission to let him return to "regular missionary work." He confided to some of us later that working under inexperienced national leaders was "too slow to get the job done." He evidently preferred doing his own thing, rather than working toward the long-range goal of indigenous leadership.

I've been grateful for good working relationships with national leaders (except one "Napoleon"). They never make me feel that I must work *under* them. It is natural for us to work side by side. They are responsible for the administration and overall planning and a good deal more. I am a teacher, trainer and counselor. But so are other, *national* staff. These roles, in the New Testament, are subordinate to local elders. But because these staff roles are more public, we often clothe them with a higher authority than the Bible ascribes.

Usually the national leaders I have worked under were younger than I. One winter in Pakistan, John, the national executive secretary, and the staff of the national movement threw a surprise birthday party for me. When my age was coyly revealed (I already knew his age), John and I burst out in merry laughter. I was exactly twice my boss's age!

At the same time, age has more authority in non-Western societies than in the West. It is not just my "weight" in age, however, that I must be careful not to throw around. There are other factors. As a woman, I try to be sensitive about working with men in strongly patriarchal societies. This "liberated woman" learned the hard way on that one. The same goes for working in strongly matriarchal societies, but with a different emphasis. Moreover, with my racial and national background, I have had to be careful not to arouse prejudice against the Chinese in certain Asian countries and against the Americans all over.

Working around these cultural sensitivities should not be merely a professional matter. Always it is another challenge to work out our discipleship under Jesus our Lord. Ninety per cent of the time, thank God, it has not been hard. But one has to keep working at it, never taking anything for granted. I make mistakes, some obvious, some not so obvious—as I later learn. They forgive me. And when they hurt me, I forgive them. And we keep going. We can do it because we are working toward the same goal. The problems are often massive, and by the grace of God we can unite in working together on them.

Through the years I have seen how the best of these national leaders love their people deeply, and yet are equally critical of their national weaknesses. They bear the same national characteristics as their compatriots. At the same time they are above these characteristics. They are true Christian patriots. I am always eager to learn more from them because I know I do not know what they know about what I need to know. Asian brothers and sisters teach me about true sacrificial living. African brothers and sisters teach me about simple personal integrity. North American brothers and sisters teach me about openness to life. European brothers and sisters teach me about careful thinking. Latin American brothers and sisters teach me about forgiveness for national humiliations. What wealth God's family members can share with each other!

Knowing When to Leave

Whenever possible our family has open house on Christmas morning, serving brunch and a bit of joy. The invitations usually say, "Come when you can, leave when you must." This may be a good guideline for the tour of missionaries. *Can* and *must* are rather tricky terms; their meaning depends on keen observation of people and the progress of the work, sensitivity to the Holy Spirit, a lot of common sense and even more faith. Some guests are confident and gracious about the right time to leave. Other guests are not sure, and sometimes neither are the hosts.

Two common mistakes in missionary practice can jeopardize a work. We can leave too soon—before the work is truly established or at least before our particular contribution to that work is completed. We may be tempted to leave prematurely under the pressure of "turning leadership over to the nationals." In such cases, a work can lose ground that has been gained by long arduous labor. Think, for example, of the tough pioneering work done now in Islamic countries. Samuel Zwemer's forty-year ministry to the Muslims saw no converts, but his faithfulness helped lay the foundation for others to carry on today.

Or we can overstay our visit. And *visit* it is. We should always remember that, as missionaries, we are guests in someone else's country. When a Czech guest was urged sincerely by his hosts to stay just a few days longer, he replied, "Guests are like fish. Nice the first day or two. Smelly after that."

The principle of "leave when you must" prevents undue dependence on the missionary and missionary resources. Resources can mean spiritual leadership. But often it means money. Some missions have imported expensive equipment and constructed modern facilities that the local churches cannot maintain without continued financial help. "Must" allows local leaders to have full freedom under God to exercise responsibility in their own national churches. Of course, they will make mistakes. But that is no reason for perpetuating ours.

We should raise questions about theological colleges or seminaries which are still mainly staffed by westerners after many years, whose denominational churches are supposedly indigenous, and where the curriculum is essentially what the professors followed when they were students. Could it be that there is an insistence on a Western type of theological training?

Gradually appearing are positive efforts to counteract this and other such tendencies. I watch with interest the work of the Theological Research and Communication Institute of South India in Bangalore.[17] The vigorous leadership is a strong combination of Indian and Western church leaders and theologians; an Oxford graduate is assistant to the national pastor in the Church of South India. It takes courage and creativity to go against traditions, and there are always detractors. But that is the way to go.

The problem of missionary visas has also been growing steadily. Governments are consistently refusing visas to professional missionaries. National political leaders want to maintain their cultural heritage which they see eroding with the import of foreign ideas and lifestyles. Some take it as an insult to have outsiders come in and virtually tell their people what to do and how to do it.

In the seven-year period that I made visits to Malaysia, I saw the mission force dwindle. A well-known mission organization began working there in the middle 1950s with 145. Today it has eight or nine. These enter as educators or have visas that are stamped "nonrenewable." Yet this very condition helped the Malaysian Christians to realize they could no longer rely on the presence and work of outside Christians. If their churches were to survive they themselves would have to raise up leaders. So in this same period, the exit of foreign missionaries has been accompanied by the rise of strong national leadership and indigenous Bible and training schools.

Generally speaking, if a missionary stays on and on in one place or position, decade after decade, we should again raise questions. In one case I know, a missionary has been doing the same thing for thirty-two years, assisting the local pastors. When his supporting church at home investigated, the missionary admitted he had a comfortable life and home and was feeling insecure about moving on or returning to the United States.

In another case, the missionary simply does not trust the national leadership. He has become possessive about the work that he has indeed labored hard to establish. He personally raised all the necessary finances from churches at home. The work has become his personal security. Take it away, and his identity would go also. Such a missionary has become a controller, not a discipler.

True missionaries are linkers, linking sinners to God, linking young disciples to Scripture and fellowship. They link disciple makers to resources that will train them better for the ministry. If they have been faithful linkers and not controllers, they can gladly commit "the elders" to the Lord in whom they all believe (Acts 14:23).

A few weeks ago I received a letter from a coworker. He has been an effective evangelist and a wise discipler. God has used him to help pioneer a healthy evangelical student movement. I was momentarily stunned to read that he had been asked to move to another country to start another kind of work. It would not be with students but with refugees, because of that particular crisis. Then as I tried to envision the whole scene, I realized that indeed it was a wise move.

He had done so well in the student ministry that he had worked himself out of a job in six years. But he has not worked himself out of his calling from God to be a missionary. His geographical location, his status, his relationships and his emphasis may change, but not his original commission from the Lord Jesus.

Ah, says someone, it is easy to raise up leaders from among students. What about the average national who is less educated? Leadership is not a matter of formal education. Every group has natural leaders. Through prayer letters, I follow the work of some Wycliffe translators in New Guinea. For years they have been diligently translating the Gospel of Mark and some primers for reading. But their ultimate goal has been to establish a church for that language group. That church has been forming. And leaders are emerging from that once illiterate group.

Once, in a West African country, friends arranged for me to stay with such a missionary family, the Bankses. Their love for the people became very clear one morning. At breakfast I was asked if I had heard any noise during the night. No, I had slept deeply. Don Banks told me that a burglar had cut the screen off the window, removed the glass louvers and taken off with a radio and some other things. I glanced around that simple home and wondered why a thief would pick that house. But what was more impressive to me was the way the parents handled the affair before their three young children. They were not angry but sympathetic with the thief who was so poor that he had to steal to get food for his starving family. As a matter of fact, they felt sorry for him because he had stolen the radio that didn't work. The children got into the act and suggested that the next time they ought to make a sign with an arrow pointing to the good radio—"This way, thief!" The result was that the children were not fearful, nor had they lost a shred of love for the townspeople.

Because of mutual love and trust between the Bankses and the local people, I was not surprised to hear a few years later that they had returned home to Britain. Don's work of heading the publishing ministry was being turned over to the Africans he had so lovingly trained.

Whether in a sophisticated city like Ephesus or a small town like Derbe off the major Roman arterial, Paul and his partners made it their aim to leave the churches they had planted as soon as they could in the hands of local elders (Acts 14:23). Our goal is to do the same.

Epilog

THE BEST SURPRISES ARE YET TO COME

OFTEN ON A MORNING I AWAKE and still marvel that I am moving on with God. That is grace. I would not exchange these years of service to our Lord for a million dollars. (Though for two million, I would forego some parts!) It has been worth every minute, even or maybe especially the hardest parts. Serious discipleship always includes them. It is not a matter of being masochistic, getting pleasure out of suffering. It is a matter of being doubly realistic— in a sinful world of sinful people, a life of holiness is not easy. But God Almighty gives us grace to live it out. This is his way of shaping and molding our character.

I began this book saying I had not been given any missionary orientation. But fellow missionaries and many overseas Christians have more than made up for the formal missionary training that

I did not have. National colleagues and others have taught me deeply about attitudes and better ways of doing God's work. They have stretched my concept of God himself. And certainly their friendships have smoothed some of my rough edges. I believe that my life and service are immeasurably richer because of them.

As soon as I arrived in Hong Kong, my first assignment overseas, I had to let go of preconceived ideas about my ministry. Student work was young in Asia. I assumed that nobody knew as much about it as I did, particularly after seven years of experience, to say nothing of my formal training. But I fell flat on my face time and time again. I was not in demand. Nor were hundreds being brought to the Lord through my ministry.

Missionaries instinctively think of themselves as superior to those they go to serve, contradictory as that sounds. For are they not preachers, teachers and evangelists with authority? Yes, but it is authority delegated from our Sovereign Lord. Moreover, we can teach only *some* things. The learners have much to teach us, especially when cultural conflicts or other kinds of tensions arise. We are fellow humans.

Who are the teachers? Who are the learners? We all are.

The first thing I learned from my Chinese colleagues in Hong Kong was teamwork. In Hawaii I had been the only staff worker. I was used to making decisions alone. Now I had to adjust to three other minds, three different temperaments and three workstyles. It was confusing and painful. How patient they were with me! I learned that working in a team led to more effective ministries for all of us. They encouraged me to develop a Bible study ministry. Now I could concentrate on doing a better job because I no longer had to do everything. I began to appreciate in a practical way what membership in the body of Christ means.

Real sacrifice was the second big lesson I learned from the wider family of coworkers in Asia. At the end of my first dreadful five months, about fifteen workers and graduates from six or seven countries gathered in Manila for the first regional staff training conference. (That was my first regional Bible study workshop, and

I discovered I had forgotten an important item—my Bible!) I thought I had made great sacrifices, leaving home and the comforts and luxuries of Hawaii. But these were peanuts compared to their sacrifices. Fellowship with these younger brothers and sisters turned me around.

All of them belonged to that first generation of university-educated Christians in the Third World (a postcolonial phenomenon). Their families had sacrificed to put them through university, hoping that they would get high-paying jobs and bring prestige to the family name with financial security. For these young people, to enter Christian service meant putting aside personal ambitions as well as sorrowfully disappointing their families. It was then that I ceased struggling about returning to Hawaii where I had felt more useful. I knew I would throw my lot in with them to pioneer more campuses in Asia.

And I learned about worship. I used to keep a file of worship ideas, hoping to improve on many dull services if ever I had the opportunity. I have thrown away that file in favor of recommending that people go to an African church service (not the westernized kind). I have not seen anything like it elsewhere. African believers have an exuberance that is difficult for many westerners to understand—we are not used to such genuinely joyous expressions. Africans sing with their whole body, their whole being. They have a sense of the awesome presence of God that we seem to have lost in the West. When the Word of God is proclaimed, their eyes are riveted on God's messenger. No other sound is heard besides his voice. (Or is it God's voice?) They present their offerings, dancing their way to the altar with singing. I am not the dancing kind, but if I am with brothers and sisters like that, my feet cannot help moving along with them in celebration of God's goodness. I have a feeling that worship before the throne of the Lamb in heaven will be more reverent and exuberant because of their presence.

These lessons were just the beginning of many more—about simple, loving hospitality, group sensitivities (long before group dynamics became popular), mutual pastoral care (long before I led workshops on that) and so on.

But there are some things that no experienced missionary or tactful national colleague can ever teach us. Some concern deep-seated attitudes that can be transformed by the Holy Spirit only through personal struggles. Others are simply a part of one's discipleship—the delightful surprises God gives us on the other side of obedience.

It took some doing for me to get rid of the notion that I would be doing God a huge favor by being his missionary. I had struggled about going overseas in the first place. I had usually overcome the arguments with the fact that I was already serving him at home. And in case he needed reminding, I wondered out loud to him if the work in Hawaii could get along without me. Of course it could. But even though I was only fifty-one per cent willing to go overseas—while the other forty-nine per cent of me balked—that was good enough for him. Had I not taken that first step of obedience, however faltering, what adventures with him I would have missed! He has been doing *me* the favor all along.

Neither IFES (International Fellowship of Evangelical Students) nor I had planned that I would have an itinerant ministry after my first assignment. Never in my wildest imagination could I have conjured up such an idea for a woman. In fact, like any woman, what I most wanted was to settle down into my own home and minister out of it, not out of a suitcase. I wanted the security of a five-year plan. I wanted to study at a spacious desk with a library at hand. With these conditions I would happily serve the Lord.

But that was not to be. Those were the years when God was establishing evangelistic student movements in every Asian country where it was politically possible. He was raising up his leaders everywhere for a new age in his churches in Asia, and they were calling for whatever help we could give them. No, IFES had no five-year plan for me, but it did have David Adeney, who was then the associate general secretary for East Asia. We were two of only three IFES staff workers in Asia. David was advance party and seed sower in new countries, trouble-shooter and counselor in emerging movements—a true Barnabas. When, in our travels, we could meet at an airport or city, he would always be ready with three or four other possible assignments. Like his namesake, David was truly "a man after God's own heart." I usually trusted his judgments and always he listened to my side of the story. For pioneering work, a relationship with such an experienced partner is far more important than a five-year plan.

Some friends think that living out of a suitcase must have been a great sacrifice for me. There have been struggles, but in my heart of hearts I had always wanted a simple lifestyle—not to be encumbered with unnecessary possessions and manners. The Lord did not force the itinerant lifestyle on me for the sake of his work. Choice of a ministry is prior to choice of a lifestyle. Or to put it another way, a lifestyle is predetermined by the choice of a ministry.

So an itinerant ministry was his creative way of helping me to work out a desire. In the late sixties, the hippies confirmed me in this lifestyle. They showed me that it is indeed possible to live with a minimum wardrobe without embarrassment. But I still like my clothes a bit cleaner than theirs. I say "a bit" cleaner, because I also have learned to be less neurotic about cleanliness.

During those years, I also gathered up some important lessons about God's gifts. The first is that one does not have to own a house in order to have a home. In every country where I have worked, God's people have opened their homes to me—parents, children and family life. Jesus said there is not one of us who has left father, mother, brothers, sisters, homes, land or children who will not be rewarded a hundredfold in this life, and in life eternal (Mk 10:29-30). I take this literally.

The second lesson is that one does not have to possess things in order to enjoy them. Obviously, I could not carry in my suitcase many things I admired—a lovely painting, a fine china dish or a wood sculpture. I learned to store their beauty in my soul the way the Japanese sit quietly smelling certain woods burning while they watch the moon rise. I learned to store greater beauties— a magnificent midcontinental evening sky, the emerald deeps and shallows near an ocean shore, a loving, loyal friendship. Keats's observation that "A thing of beauty is a joy forever" applies also to the images of beauty in our minds.

A few years ago I moved to England to be Bible-study secretary for IFES. For the first time in my life I had a home of my own (temporarily), thanks to some very kind friends. The spacious flat was ideal as a home base for my continuing travels, and most helpful for overseas friends coming to London. There was a lovely garden in the back, full of flowers and fruit in their season. I could hardly believe that the Lord would be that good to me. Then one day I realized with even deeper gratitude that God had taught me well. For deep within me I knew that if he should some day change the circumstances, I could live contentedly without that lovely flat with its lovely furnishings. As it turned out, he did and I could. That's the kind of God we serve. His gift of contentment is one of his better gifts.

I spoke earlier of how important it is for missionaries to plan ahead for what they will do after their final overseas assignment. Few of us in this new era of international mission work should expect to end our earthly days or even our earthly service overseas. Many missionaries return home and spend the rest of their life feeling like a has-been—an old hymnal catching dust on a church shelf. That is not Jesus' kind of discipleship. If any of us have anything to do with mission work at home or overseas, we ought to give more loving thought and action to this problem.

Coming home does not end our missionary calling. If anything, that calling should be enhanced. When Jesus returned home to his Father, his calling was greatly expanded. He is constantly interceding for us and is working mightily by his Holy Spirit to continue that mission. I used to dream of what my last assignment on earth might be. My basic dream was to have a more settled base where I could (1) team up with others for lay training in local churches, (2) keep in vital touch with God's global mission as well as visit old friends and coworkers and (3) somehow serve as a link between these two worlds by working with others to prepare more disciples for that worldwide mission. It was just another one of my many wild dreams. A few months ago when I returned to Hawaii for family reasons, I discovered in a matter of weeks that God had already been at work on that wild dream.

I have already begun a new ministry in Hawaii, where I first began serving God. I have come full circle, back to a ministry of lay training in local churches. Only this time I feel better qualified. Moreover, God had been preparing several others who have had the same wild dreams. As a team, we have started to put into reality the accumulated lessons God has been teaching us through the years about living and working with him and his people. And part of this ministry is periodically to visit and help in God's work overseas. What a God we serve!

In the end, however, what really matters is not how many countries we have worked in, or what important or exotic people we have met. It is not how many books we have written or how creative our teaching and training courses can be. God is far more interested in what is happening to us inside. Are we becoming more like Jesus Christ, his Son? That is what counts in the end (Rom 8:29).

Discipleship is a constant moving forward to any new assignment the Lord gives. Every one he has given me so far has been exciting and exhilarating, full of adventure and surprises. Obedience on earth expands our capacities to enjoy heaven and the king of heaven. Having come this far with him, I know the best surprises are yet to come.

Notes

[1]*The Illustrated Bible Dictionary,* ed. (Leicester: Inter-Varsity Press, 1980), p. 40.

[2]Knowing the earthly life of Jesus Christ is the concrete basis for following him. It takes time to travel this road, in fact a whole lifetime. But like any other journey, it begins with the first step. Begin that journey with a friend or two who also wish to follow Jesus in a more consistent way. Commit yourselves to one another for regular studies together. If you are not used to this kind of personal Bible study, you may want to use a guide. There are so many good guides for any of the Gospels that I dare not recommend any one. Almost any guide is better than none. Keep a commentary and a Bible dictionary handy, but do not study these. Study the Bible!

More important than Bible study aids is the set of equipment God has already built into you. Learn to (1) use your powers of observation of the text, (2) ask proper questions of the text and yourself, (3) take time to reflect on the meaning of the text, and most of all (4) be willing to obey its practical implications.

Here are some specific pointers to get you started. Watch Jesus as he interacts with people. What seems to be the purpose for his actions? What attitudes and qualities of character emerge? Note how people respond to him. Why? What is unique about their situation? What does Jesus see in them that others do not? What do you learn about human nature? Trace repeated ideas or related activities. What trends and patterns do you observe? Reflect on Jesus' person. What is provoking about him in this event? How should this truth affect your life? your fellowship? your community?

[3]Dr. LeRoy N. Johnston, Jr., "Should I Be a Missionary?" *Journal of Psychology and Christianity* 2, no. 4 (Winter 1983).

[4]Some of our Latin brothers and sisters are not entirely happy with the word *training.* The association with the training of animals is apparently too strong. *Training* can connote mechanical conditioning. The happier choice in French and Spanish is *formation* and *formación* respectively. Even in English, *formation* connotes the development of moral character. Nevertheless, we will continue to use the word *training* in this book, understanding that it means this kind of character formation.

[5]A. B. Bruce's *The Training of the Twelve* (New Canaan, Connecticut: Keats, 1979) forced me to re-examine the four Gospels. First published in 1871, it is a classic on this subject.

[6]Discipleship Training Centre, 33-A Chancery Lane, Singapore 11. Asian Bible Center, c/o UESI, P.O. Box 1030, Madras 600-010, India.

[7]S. J. Palmer, *Korea and Christianity* (Seoul: Hollym Corp., 1967).

[8]P. J. Johnstone, *A Handbook for World Intercession* (Bromley, England: STL Publications, 1978), p. 115.

[9]Ibid., p. 147.

[10]According to Dr. Stanley E. Lindquist, these statistics and the problems they represent are comparable to overseas employees of secular organizations returning home in the *first* year ("Prediction of Success in Overseas Adjustment," *Journal of Psychology and Christianity* 1, no. 2 [Summer 1982]). Dr. Lindquist is the president of Link Care Foundation (Fresno, CA), which is dedicated to a program of missionary adjustments. They are interviewing mission boards and secular organizations, such as the Peace Corps, the U.S. Navy, and the Canadian Foreign Service. Working out a better screening and orientation process is their main task. No mission board, according to their research so far, claims satisfaction with their present system. We can pray with them that their work may reduce the number of missionary dropouts in the years ahead.

[11]R. Pierce Beaver, "The History of Mission Strategy," *Southwestern Journal of Theology* 12, no. 2 (Spring 1970). This article is included in Ralph D. Winter and Stephen C. Hawthorne, eds., *Perspectives on the World Christian Movement: A Reader* (Pasadena: William Carey Library, 1981), p. 203.

[12]If I find that a passage seems to contradict other parts of biblical teaching, as in the case of a traditional reading of 1 Timothy 2:12, then I use these three principles of interpretation: (1) I look carefully at the meaning of the key words and their relationship to ideas in the preceding and following verses. In this case, they are *permit, a woman [or wife], to have [full] authority, men [or husbands]*. What did Paul mean when he used these words/terms in that grammatical context? (2) I try to ascertain the historical context to which these were addressed. In this case, Paul was instructing Timothy amidst his pastoral problems in licentious pagan Ephesus, where there were many false teachers, and some (typically uneducated but eager) women were getting out of hand. So I must ask, Is this a universal principle or a specific situation (from which we may nevertheless derive a practical principle for today)? We should ask this of 1 Timothy 5:23 as well as of 1 Timothy 2:12. (3) I interpret the unclear passage with what is clear elsewhere in the Bible, for the Word of God is harmonious. In this case, the *progressive trend* of women leading and teaching begins at least as early as Miriam in Exodus, Deborah in Judges 4—5 and Huldah in 2 Kings

22:14. Then the trend *increases in frequency* through Acts and the Pauline letters, especially as evidenced in Romans 16. Capping this progressive trend back to Genesis 1:26-28 is the clear doctrinal statement of Galatians 3:28-29: "There is neither Jew nor Greek, slave nor free, male nor female, for you are all one in Christ Jesus. If you belong to Christ, then you are Abraham's seed, and heirs according to the promise."

[13]Tim Dowley, ed., *The History of Christianity* (Hertsfordshire, England: Lion Publishing, 1977), pp. 520-21.

[14]*Christian Brethren Review Journal,* no. 33 (1982). The entire issue is devoted to "Women in the Church."

[15]When the term *Third World* originated after World War 2, it referred to the politically neutral countries not aligned with either the First World (the West) or the Second World (the communist countries). More often today, people have in mind the emerging nations that are economically still developing, usually in the Southern Hemisphere. In an attempt to be accurate without sounding superior or condescending, the following terms are also used: emerging nations, developing nations, young nations and Two-Thirds World.

[16]It is not easy to keep up with the rapid changes in world missions. We should remember that world politics are usually reflected in mission changes. Periodicals like the *International Bulletin of Missionary Research* (Ventnor, New Jersey) help me to keep somewhat abreast. I glance over the more academic articles to see what the missiologists are now worrying about. Then I concentrate on one or two articles relating to my current practical concerns. I always read the book reviews.

[17]"Urbana" refers to the student missions convention of Inter-Varsity Christian Fellowship held every three years at the University of Illinois at Urbana.

[18]132 St. John's Church Road, Bangalore, 560005, India.